Test Your Vocabulary – Book 5 (Advanced)

Peter Watcyn-Jones

Illustrated by Terry Burton

D1293636

PENGUIN ENGLISH

PENGUIN BOOKS

Published by the Penguin Group
Penguin Books Ltd, 27 Wrights Lane, London W8 5TZ, England
Viking Penguin, a division of Penguin Books USA Inc.
375 Hudson Street, New York, New York 10014, USA
Penguin Books Australia Ltd, Ringwood, Victoria, Australia
Penguin Books Canada Ltd, 2801 John Street, Markham, Ontario, Canada L3R 1B4
Penguin Books (NZ) Ltd, 182–190 Wairau Road, Auckland 10, New Zealand

Penguin Books Ltd, Registered Offices: Harmondsworth, Middlesex, England

First published 1991
10 9 8 7 6 5 4 3 2 1

Filmset in Century Schoolbook

Made and printed in Great Britain by
BPCC Hazell Books
Aylesbury, Bucks, England
Member of BPCC Ltd.

INTRODUCTION

TEST YOUR VOCABULARY – Book 5 (Advanced) is the latest addition to the *Test Your Vocabulary* series and was written in response to a request for a more advanced book than Book 4. It is suitable for students following any advanced course of study (e.g. Cambridge Proficiency) and can even be used by native speakers for revision purposes.

There are fifty tests altogether and, like the previous books in the series, the emphasis is on variety, with tests ranging from multiple-choice exercises to tests on synonyms, verbs, adjectives, idioms and phrasal verbs. In addition there are crosswords, newspaper misprints, homophones, and so on. Altogether there are approximately 1,500 words.

TEST YOUR VOCABULARY – Book 5 (Advanced) can be used in class with a teacher or for self-study. To facilitate the latter, a key is included.

In writing this book, I have consulted a number of different dictionaries. The following can be warmly recommended:

Longman Dictionary of Contemporary English – new edition (Longman)
Collins Cobuild Essential English Dictionary (Collins)
Oxford Advanced Learners Dictionary (Oxford University Press)
The Penguin Wordmaster Dictionary, Manser and Turton (Penguin)

TO THE STUDENT

This book will help you to learn a lot of new English words. But in order for the new words to become "fixed" in your mind, you need to test yourself again and again. Here is one method you can use to help you learn the words.

1. Read through the instructions carefully for the test you are going to try. Then try the test, writing your answers **in pencil**.
2. When you have finished, check your answers and correct any mistakes you have made. Read through the test again, paying special attention to the words you didn't know or got wrong.
3. Try the test again five minutes later. You can do this either by covering up the words or by asking a friend to test you. Repeat this until you can remember all the words.
4. **Rub out your answers**.
5. Try the test again the following day. (You should remember most of the words.)
6. Finally, plan to try the test at least twice again within the following month. After this most of the words will be "fixed" in your mind.

CONTENTS

Words of similar meaning: Adjectives

Complete each of the groups of three words with a word that is similar in meaning. Choose from the following:

belligerent	destitute	irate	ravenous
clamorous	discrepant	obese	slothful
copious	fervent	opulent	stingy
coy	frugal	paltry	valiant
cumbersome	impetuous	perilous	wily

1   angry, furious, livid ...

2   aggressive, militant, hostile ...

3   brave, courageous, intrepid ...

4   bulky, clumsy, unwieldy ...

5   cunning, artful, sly ...

6   dangerous, hazardous, risky ...

7   eager, keen, zealous ...

8   economical, sparing, thrifty ...

9   fat, portly, corpulent ...

10   noisy, boisterous, vociferous ...

11   hasty, rash, impulsive ...

12   hungry, starving, famished ...

13   incongruous, incompatible, incoherent ...

14   lazy, idle, indolent ...

15   mean, tight-fisted, miserly ...

16   broke, penniless, skint ...

17   plentiful, abundant, bountiful ...

18   rich, wealthy, affluent ...

19   shy, sheepish, bashful ...

20   unimportant, petty, trivial ...

2 Group nouns/Collective nouns

Fill in the missing words.

1 a .... of endurance   F _ _ _

2 a .... of lions   P _ I _

3 a .... of events   _ _ R I _

4 a .... of luck   _ _ R _ K _

5 a .... of dancers   _ R O _ _ _

6 an .... of poems   A _ T H _ _ _ _

7 a .... of treatment   _ _ _ R S _

8 a .... of tunes   M _ _ _ _ Y

9 a .... of bacon   _ _ S H _ R

10 a .... of dry weather   _ _ _ _ L L

11 a .... of notes (= money)   W _ _

12 an .... of nerves   _ T T _ _ _

13 a .... of short stories   C _ _ L _ _ T _ _ _

14 a .... of arrows   Q _ _ V _ _

15 a .... of meat   _ _ _ N T _

16 a .... of grass   _ _ _ F _

17 a .... of red hair   S _ _ _ K

18 a .... of fresh air   _ _ _ _ _ T H

19 a .... of sand   _ _ A _ N

20 a .... of land   _ _ _ _ T _

21 a .... of dust   _ P _ C _

22 a .... of imprisonment   `T | | |`

23 a .... of ants   `| | L | | Y`

24 a .... of whales   `| C | H | | |`

25 an .... of news   `| T | |`

26 a .... of motorway   `S | R | | | H`

27 a .... of trees   `| L | | P |`

28 a .... of thunder   `| L | |`

29 a .... of concrete   `B | | | K |`

30 a .... of emergency   `| T | T |`

31 an .... of clothing   `| R | T | | | E`

32 a .... of lightning   `| L | S |`

33 a .... of geese   `| | G | G | |`

34 a .... of experts   `| | N | L`

35 a .... of laughter   `| O | |`

36 a .... of locusts   `P | | G | |`

3

3 Too many words 1

Replace the words in bold type in the following sentences with a single word. (The first letter of the word is given.)

1 My brother is **able to use both hands equally well**.
   (a.................)

2 The passengers **went ashore** at Harwich.
   (d.................)

3 These computers are **completely out-of-date** now.
   (o.................)

4 **A great deal of** damage was caused by the earthquake.
   (E.................)

5 One side of a postage stamp is **covered with a sticky substance**.
   (a.................)

6 The two countries signed an **agreement to stop fighting**.
   (a.................)

7 Your actions may have **put** our plans **in danger**.
   (j................. our plans)

8 The meeting was **put off** until later in the week.
   (a.................)

9 The soldier was accused of **lack of courage** in the face of the enemy.
   (c.................)

10 This month's sales figures have **gone beyond** our expectations.
   (e.................)

11 The river **curves and winds** through the Wye Valley.
   (m.................)

12 My father has just got a new pair of **false teeth**.
   (d.................)

13 The fortress was **impossible to be taken by force**.
   (i.................)

14 He was found guilty of **murdering his mother**.
   (m.................)

15 The margin of error is **so small that it can be ignored**.
   (n.................)

16 At least twenty villages were **laid waste** by the floods.
(d..................)

17 Some of the planes were no longer **fit to fly**.
(a..................)

18 He is suffering from **loss of memory**.
(a..................)

19 We tried to **find out** the cause of the accident.
(a..................)

20 His appetite for power and wealth is **impossible to satisfy**.
(i..................)

4 Missing words: Adjectives

Fill in the missing adjectives in the sentences below. Choose from the following:

adamant	eligible	indigenous	requisite
avid	exorbitant	inopportune	sedentary
circumstantial	feasible	irrevocable	slushy
commensurate	heinous	petty	spontaneous
congested	implicated	plausible	squeamish
cursory	implicit	prevailing	unanimous
dishevelled	incessant	prolific	vivid
	indicative	redundant	

1 Brian wasn't really interested in art, so he gave each painting no more than a .... glance.

2 "You have been found guilty of a most .... crime," said the judge.

3 The kangaroo and koala bear are .... to Australia.

4 The .... cash is kept in that black box over there.

5 I could never watch an operation; I'm far too .... I even faint when someone has a nosebleed.

6 My parents were .... about not letting me go to the pop concert.

7 The plan sounds .... , but I'd like to discuss it with the others before giving you the go-ahead.

8 As a child I had .... faith in my parents. As far as I was concerned, they could do no wrong.

9 There's nothing you can do, I'm afraid. The committee's decision is ....

10 He gave a very .... excuse for being late.

11 To go to university you have to have the .... number of A-levels.

12 Now that it had started to thaw, the roads were very ....

13 To be a writer, you need among other things a .... imagination.

14 Even as a child she was a(n) .... reader.

15 You could tell she had only just got out of bed. She had no make-up on and her hair was ....

16 Do you think any other members of the Government are .... in the current scandals?

17 The .... noise from the workmen outside my window was beginning to drive me mad.

18 People with .... jobs ought to get as much exercise as possible in their free time.

19 The board members gave .... support to the proposal.

20 The police didn't have any definite proof that he had committed the crime; all the evidence was ....

21 Only single people are .... to join this club.

22 The fact that only 40 per cent turned out to vote in the election is .... of the state of political apathy in the country at present.

23 The .... wind in this area is from the west.

24 Nothing Peter says or does is ever .... He always thinks things out very carefully beforehand.

25 She was looking for a job .... with her abilities.

26 We didn't buy anything because we thought the prices were ....

27 She arrived at a most .... moment; I was just getting into the shower.

28 She was a .... writer who averaged fifteen to twenty books a year.

29 I hate driving through London because the streets are so ....

30 When the car factory closed down, more than 2,000 workers were made ....

Cartoons

In the following cartoons, the captions have got mixed up, so that each cartoon has been printed with the wrong caption under it. Work out the correct caption for each cartoon.

Cartoon		Correct caption	Cartoon		Correct caption
1	–	....	6	–	....
2	–	....	7	–	....
3	–	....	8	–	....
4	–	....	9	–	....
5	–	....	10	–	....

1 I think I'd better explain the term "free kick".

2 No thanks, I've already got four.

3 Why didn't you tell me one of your arms was shorter than the other?

4 Try not to laugh, Dorothy, it will only encourage him to be naughty.

5 I just popped in to see how the novel's coming on.

6 For goodness sake let him have it, Albert. It's only a worm!

7 I wonder if you'd mind pronouncing that again, sir.

8 Now see if you can guess what tune I'm playing this time.

9 The interviewer asked me what I was good at, so I nutted him.

10 I think I've got it, Simpkins. It says "mind the step".

6 Word association

Write next to each of the words on the left a word that can be associated with it. Choose from the words on the right. Use each word once only.

1   apple ....

2   athletics ....

3   bicycle ....

4   billiards ....

5   book ....

6   candle ....

7   car ....

8   chimney ....

9   church ....

10 clock ....

11 comb ....

12 cow ....

13 cricket ....

14 ear ....

15 fish ....

16 flower ....

17 funeral ....

18 hair ....

19 horse ....

20 jacket ....

21 ladder ....

22 nut ....

23 piano ....

24 prostitute ....

25 river ....

26 roof ....

27 ship ....

28 shirt ....

29 telephone ....

30 violin ....

bonnet

bridge

core

cuff

cushion

estuary

flue

funnel

gills

hammer

hand

handset

jacket

kernel

lapel

lobe

mane

parting

pimp

pulpit

rafter

relay

rung

spoke

stem

tooth

udder

umpire

wick

wreath

7 Verbal expressions

Fill in the missing verbs below. Choose from the following (use each verb once only):

acquire	cook	fill	keep	read
alleviate	cut	follow	lead	see
bear	draw	form	lose	serve
call	drive	hang	make	take
collect	drop	hold	play	throw

1   To .... a conclusion

2   To .... suit

3   To .... allowances

4   To .... a party

5   To .... a taste for something

6   To .... someone a line

7   To .... wallpaper

8   To .... between the lines

9   To .... suffering

10 To .... one's thoughts

11 To .... the fort

12 To .... stars

13 To .... a grudge against someone

14 To .... the books

15 To .... a vacancy

16 To .... truant

17 To .... precautions

18 To .... someone's bluff

19 To .... a hard bargain

20 To .... a company

21 To .... time

22 To .... a tooth

23 To .... house

24 To .... heart

25 To .... someone up the garden path

Sort out the clues 1

Look at the completed crossword below. See if you can work out which word goes with which clue. Write 1 Across, 15 Down, etc., in front of each clue. (See example)

1 Across to search and steal

.... to walk at an easy, gentle pace

.... to steal in small amounts

.... living both on land and in water

.... learned, scholarly

.... a two-hundredth anniversary

.... an inscription on a tomb

.... one of the signs of the Zodiac

.... a loud whistle or cry expressing disapproval or displeasure at the theatre, a sports match, etc.

.... to fall like a waterfall

.... short-lived, lasting only a day or so

.... talkative, wordy

.... extremely overweight

.... a task that is unpleasant or boring

.... wreckage found floating on the surface of the sea

.... a kind of chicory, used as salad

.... to idle, loiter, waste time

.... to defer, delay in doing some necessary act

.... imprisoned, confined

.... slightly hungry

.... a natural sleep of some animals throughout the winter

.... a word or sentence that reads the same backwards and forwards

.... to listen secretly to a private conversation

.... to separate by cutting

.... prone to anger, irritable

.... at the point of death, dying

.... a list of prices and charges

.... a type of small flying insect (like a mosquito) that bites people

.... a sweet-smelling garden flower

.... smuggled goods

9 Multiple-choice 1

Choose the word or phrase which best completes each sentence.

1 The accused man was proved innocent and was ....

   a liberated   **b** excused   **c** interned   **d** acquitted

2 There was a very suspicious character .... in the shadows.

   a lurking   **b** peeping   **c** peering   **d** awaiting

3 For a moment it was difficult to see through the .... of the headlights.

   a shimmer   **b** glare   **c** glow   **d** glaze

4 Richard Burton was noted for his clear .... of words.

   a enunciation   **b** interpretation   **c** announcement
   d accentuation

5 It .... rains whenever I go out without my umbrella.

   a continually   **b** invariably   **c** typically   **d** infallibly

6 Don't waste your time telling Janet a joke; she's totally .... of a sense of humour.

   a deficient   **b** missing   **c** devoid   **d** lacking

7 The old man's .... body presented a really pitiful picture.

   a flimsy   **b** lanky   **c** sparse   **d** emaciated

8 When he accidentally hit his thumb with a hammer, he let out .... which could be heard half-way down the street.

   a swearing   **b** a cursor   **c** a squeak   **d** an expletive

9 The photocopier in our office needs a complete .... These copies are terrible.

   a maintenance   **b** repair   **c** overhaul   **d** renovation

10 A prominent member of the Cabinet was .... as correspondent in the divorce case.

   a cited   **b** included   **c** accused   **d** linked

11 She was a wonderful talker. She really had the gift of the ....

   a bard   **b** words   **c** gab   **d** Gods

12 Because of their upbringing, most British men are too .... to cry.

    a restrained   **b** inhibited   **c** stiff   **d** controlled

13 Technology is advancing so rapidly nowadays that computers and other machines seem to be .... after a very short time.

    a antiquated   **b** irreparable   **c** disused   **d** obsolete

14 He didn't speak a word of French when he first moved to France. He had to pick up the language from ....

    a scratch   **b** start   **c** nought   **d** nil

15 We decided to .... the decision to a later meeting.

    a adjourn   **b** cancel   **c** defer   **d** suspend

16 After travelling all day, he was completely ....

    a done in   **b** done up   **c** broken down   **d** used up

17 I can't tell you very much about the subject, I'm afraid. I only have a very .... knowledge of it myself.

    a fundamental   **b** primary   **c** elemental   **d** rudimentary

18 Any aggressive act on their part now would be .... to war.

    a tantamount   **b** parallel   **c** commensurate   **d** comparable

19 The police tried in vain to persuade the journalist to .... the source of her information.

    a release   **b** divulge   **c** expose   **d** admit

20 When Gerald Ford became President of the U.S.A. he used his .... to pardon his predecessor, Richard Nixon.

    a influence   **b** prerogative   **c** authorities   **d** potency

21 The travel agency sent us a detailed .... of our journey to India.

    a docket   **b** agenda   **c** itinerary   **d** documentation

22 Since our train leaves at 10.30, it is .... that everyone is at the station no later than 10.15.

    a imperative   **b** urgent   **c** desired   **d** inescapable

10 Newspaper misprints 1

In each of the following extracts from a newspaper there is a misprint. Underline the word which is wrong and also write down which word should have been used instead.

Example: The 40-year-old man has dark hair with a prominent <u>fridge</u>. (..**fringe**..)

1 The will disposes of a million-dollar estate, the bunk going to relatives. (.................)

2 Why rend your garments elsewhere when our up-to-date laundry can do the work more effectively? (.................)

3 CLOTHES BRUSH: The genuine pigskin back opens with a zip and inside are tweezers, scissors, nail file and a bomb. (.................)

4 Mrs Wilson has a fine, fair skin which, she admits ruefully, comes out in a mass of freckles at the first hint of sin. (.................)

5 FOR SALE: Three bra electric fire. Perfect condition. £40. (.................)

6 She used an ordinary casting rod and a light tickle. (.................)

7 Simon Grove, as a woebegone tramp, has a bedpan manner that is often very funny. (.................)

8 He was Chairman of Berwickshire Hunt Committee from March 1968. He rode regularly to hounds until his death would not allow him to do so any more. (.................)

9 On Monday, Councillor Brown's daughter will be married to the eldest son of Councillor Jones. The members of the Corporation are invited to the suspicious event. (.................)

10 Mary and Jack Cohen thank the Almighty for their recovery. They wish to express their deepest gratitude to the many friends for great help during the time. "Good friends are priceless germs." (.................)

11 Lliw Valley development committee have been told that the coming Celtic Sea oil boob is sure to bring many benefits to the area. (.................)

12 This week's special Sunday lunch: Soup of the day, fruit juice, melon, ribs of beef, fresh local roast chicken and stuffed pork lion. (.................)

13 Eric Simpson, Stoke's 36-year-old defender, has been given a free transfer. He played only four first team games this season after struggling for long spells with knee and thing injury. (.................)

14 At a presentation held in the village church, Mrs Jones was given a tea-set and a travelling rub by the vicar. (.................)

15 British Airways shop stewards met today in a bid to resolve a dispute which has strangled thousands of passengers at Heathrow. (.................)

16 She was married in Evansville, Indiana, to Walter Jackson, and to this onion was born three children. (.................)

17 To make a piece of boiled bacon really delicious, add to the water a teaspoonful of vinegar, a small bit of nutmeg, and a couple of gloves. (....................)

18 Mr and Mrs David Hughes of Swansea are announcing the approaching marriage of their daughter Megan to Mr Brian Williams. The couple will exchange cows on Saturday September 28th. (....................)

19 Before Miss Jenkins concluded the concert by singing "I'll Walk Beside You" she was prevented with a bouquet of red roses. (....................)

20 BUSINESS LADY requires comfortable bed-sitting room with boar. (....................)

11 Words of similar meaning: Verbs

Complete each of the groups of three words with a word that is similar in meaning. Choose from the following:

abhor	coerce	jibe	scurry
abridge	corroborate	pillage	shelve
allure	crow	postulate	snicker
bicker	dupe	procure	thwart
chide	fathom	revere	vex

1   abbreviate, shorten, condense ....

2   acquire, gain, obtain ....

3   admire, respect, venerate ....

4   annoy, bother, pester ....

5   argue, quarrel, squabble ....

6   assume, suppose, infer ....

7   brag, boast, swagger ....

8   cheat, swindle, hoodwink ....

9   confirm, verify, affirm ....

10 force, compel, oblige ....

11 hate, detest, loathe ....

12 laugh, chuckle, guffaw ....

13 oppose, resist, withstand ....

14 postpone, adjourn, put off ....

15 rebuke, scold, reprimand ....

16 rush, scamper, dash ....

17 sneer, scoff, jeer ....

18 tempt, entice, seduce ....

19 understand, comprehend, grasp ....

20 rob, steal, plunder ....

12 True or False?

Choose whether you think the following sentences are correct or not by writing the words "True" or "False" in the appropriate column.

		True	False
1	A person who collects stamps is called a **philatelist**.	....	....
2	You usually buy strawberries in a **punnet**.	....	....
3	**Penultimate** means last.	....	....
4	A **trilby** is something you wear.	....	....
5	A **cantankerous** person would make very good company.	....	....
6	A **catkin** is a female kitten.	....	....
7	**Scotch mist** is a type of drink.	....	....
8	Another word for attic is **loft**.	....	....
9	A **ferret** is a type of bird.	....	....
10	**Manure** is good for the garden.	....	....
11	"You can't see me – I'm **invincible!**"	....	....
12	A **crony** is an old, close friend.	....	....
13	You would probably feel flattered if someone described you as a **pervert**.	....	....
14	**Biennial** means "twice a year".	....	....
15	A **budgie** is a popular pet in Britain.	....	....
16	A **barge** is a type of boat.	....	....
17	A female sheep is called a **ewe**.	....	....
18	A **dais** is something you stand on.	....	....
19	If you have **halitosis** you have trouble with your feet.	....	....
20	The **nadir** is the highest point of something.	....	....
21	**Spokes** are found on a bicycle.	....	....
22	A **dipstick** is used to locate water hidden underground.	....	....
23	Most people enjoy having a **chinwag** with their friends.	....	....
24	**Brisket** is beef cut from the chest of the animal.	....	....
25	You can go to a **turf accountant** if you want advice about your lawn.	....	....

13 Words that begin with "ST-"

Read through the clues/definitions and fill in the missing words, all of which begin with "st-".

1   (of a style of writing or speaking) very formal and unnatural
    `S T _ _ T _ _`

2   the metal loop attached to a horse's saddle, which you place your foot in when you are riding
    `S T _ _ R U _`

3   a classroom can become this if you never open any windows
    `S T _ _ _ Y`

4   a st.................... activity involves a lot of effort and energy
    `S T _ N U _ _ S`

5   not developing or growing; inactive
    `S T _ G _ _ _ T`

6   the right side of a ship
    `S T _ B _ _ _ D`

7   a strong, unpleasant smell
    `S T _ K`

8   someone who is in a st.................... is almost unconscious
    `S T _ P _ _`

9   the seats in the front part of a theatre directly in front of the stage
    `S T _ _ L _`

10 the main upright part of a plant
    `S T _ K`

11 a heavy vehicle used for flattening road surfaces
    `S T _ _ _ _ L L _ _`

12 the base of a tree left after the rest has been cut down
    `S T _ M _`

13 a st.................... sound or voice is very loud and unpleasant
    `S T _ _ D _ N _`

14 fixed or controlled by law
    `S T _ _ U _ _ Y`

15 quiet and secret; trying to be unseen
    `S T _ _ L _ Y`

16 if people st.................... things, they store large quantities of them for future use
    `S T _ C K _ _ E`

17 someone who is st.................... is very mean
    `S T _ _ G _`

20

18 to bend the head and shoulders forward and down

S	T			P

19 (of food) thick, heavy and sticky

S	T		D		

20 a way of standing

S	T		C	

21 You use this to carry a sick or injured person

S	T			T	C		

22 a type of cheese

S	T		L		O	

23 someone who is st................... is serious, dull and rather old-fashioned

S	T		I	

24 a common European bird with greenish-black feathers

S	T		R	L			

25 a st.................... person is short, slightly fat but strong and solid

S	T			K	

Sort out the three jokes

The three jokes below are all mixed up. See if you can sort them out. Mark the first joke 1–10, the second one 11–18 and the third one 19–27. (The first part of each joke is already marked.)

○ you had a large win on the pools – say over three hundred and fifty thousand pounds?"
"Why," replied the old lady, "I'd

○ fight. But I still think it's a funny looking dog."
"Yes," agreed the owner. "And it

○ accepted the bet and the labrador was led in to fight. After twenty-five seconds the labrador lay

○ charge. And he can provide a suitable set almost immediately."
The Englishman couldn't believe his luck and gladly

○ accepted the Scotsman's offer.
The Scotsman left the restaurant and returned ten minutes later with a pair of

○ come as too much of a shock for her.
"I think we had better

○ "That's a stupid looking dog you've got there. Can it fight?"
"Sure,"

○ false teeth which he handed to the Englishman.
"Fantastic!" exclaimed the Englishman, trying the teeth. "They

(11) It was one of the strangest looking dogs they had ever seen at the pub, and the

○ football pools.
"Tell me," said the doctor, "what would you do if

○ not a dentist," replied the Scotsman. "He's an undertaker."

○ situation was explained to him.
"Now, you don't have to worry about anything," said the doctor. "I am fully trained in such delicate matters and I feel sure I can

○ flew out of his mouth and dropped to the floor, where they broke at the feet of the Scotsman.
"Don't worry, sir,"

22

1

Grandma was nearly ninety years of age when she won £375,000 on the football pools. Her family were extremely

said the Scotsman. "My brother will soon get you a new pair and at far less cost than an English dentist would

safe if left to me."
The doctor went in to see the old lady and gradually brought the conversation around to

worried about her heart and feared that the news of her large win would

call in the doctor to tell her the news," suggested the eldest son.
The doctor soon arrived and the

regulars found it a great topic of conversation.
Eventually one of them sidled over to the dog's owner and said,

severe burst of coughing and sneezing – and he sneezed so violently that his false teeth

looked even funnier until I shaved its mane off."

replied the owner.
"Well," said the man, "I bet you £10 that my labrador can beat your dog."
The owner

break this news to her gently. I assure you, there is absolutely no need for you to fear for her health. Everything will be quite

dead on the floor. The loser, looking down at his dead dog, shook his head sadly and said, "Your dog can certainly

fit perfectly. Your brother must be a very clever dentist."
"Oh, he's

19

The Englishman was in a restaurant in Scotland when he was suddenly attacked by a

give half of it to you, of course."
The doctor fell down dead with shock.

15 Nouns from phrasal verbs

Complete each of the following sentences.

Example: Although I have flown hundreds of times, I still feel very nervous –
especially just before the **take-**......**off**....... .

1 The **on**.................... of the disease is marked by a high temperature and a
feeling of nausea.

2 The start of the tennis match had to be delayed for half an hour because of a
sudden **down**.................... .

3 The final **out**.................... of the talks between the Union and the employers is
not yet known.

4 I didn't feel like cooking, so I decided to get something from the Indian
take.................... instead.

5 There was a twenty-minute **hold-**.................... at the start of the concert
owing to technical problems with the lighting.

6 The factory's daily **out**.................... has increased by more than 25 per cent in
the past six months.

7 The President denied that he had been involved in the recent **cover-**
....

8 One of the main **draw**.................... of living in Brighton and working in
London is that you have to spend so much time in travelling every day.

9 According to a Government spokesman, further **cut**.................... in the public
sector are to be expected.

10 Her father was an ex-sergeant-major in the army. Consequently, she had a
very strict **up**.................... .

11 The car was a complete **write-**.................... after the accident.

12 This is the fifth **break-**.................... in the area in the past month, but the
police still have no idea who is doing it.

13 Traffic-jams in the town centre have been reduced dramatically since the
new **by-**.................... was opened.

14 The play got a very bad **write-**.................... in the paper. I was very surprised
as I thought it was really good.

15 This is the third **out**.................... of the disease in the past year.

16 The police are on the **look**.................... for two men suspected of robbing a
department store in the centre of town recently.

17 No one was really surprised at the **break**.................... of their marriage. They
had never really seemed very happy together.

18 The company has experienced a large number of **set**.................... in recent
years.

19 The latest traffic news is that there is an eight-mile **tail**................... on the M4.

20 Our total **out**................... in the project was £3,500.

21 Scientists last night announced a major **break**................... in the treatment of cancer.

22 I have to go to the doctor for a **check**................... next week.

23 I read in the newspaper this morning that Pele – you know, the famous Brazilian football player – is thinking of making a **come**................... .

24 There's a meeting this afternoon with the architects to discuss the **lay**................... of the new factory.

25 From the **out**................... we knew that the plan was doomed to failure.

26 The thieves made their **get**................... in a stolen post office van.

27 Wine, women and horse-racing were my cousin's **down**................... .

28 There has been a steady **build-**................... of Chinese troops along the Russian border in the past few weeks.

29 There was a very good **turn**................... at the recent union meeting. At least 85 per cent of the members were present.

30 I apologise for my **out**................... just now. I don't know what came over me. I don't usually lose my temper.

31 The firm had an annual **turn**................... of almost two billion pounds.

32 The **out**................... for the future is not very bright, I'm afraid.

33 The college was very popular and had an annual **in**................... of nearly a thousand students.

34 There was a public **out**................... when the Government announced it was going to raise income-tax by more than 10 per cent.

35 We were feeling tired after driving for several hours, so we pulled in to a **lay-**................... for a rest.

16 Missing words: Types of people 1

Fill in the missing words in the definitions below. Choose from the following:

accomplice	bursar	gossip	shop steward
agnostic	castaway	hermit	sibling
alien	compatriot	hooligan	swindler
arbitrator	conscript	midwife	toddler
artisan	copywriter	peer	tycoon
assessor	culprit	picket	underwriter
beneficiary	despot	predecessor	ward
	envoy	registrar	

1 A(n) .... is someone who has been shipwrecked.

2 A(n) .... is a person who enjoys talking about other people's private lives.

3 A(n) .... is a nurse who has been specially trained to advise pregnant women and to assist them when giving birth.

4 A(n) .... is a member of a trade union who is elected by the other members in the factory or office where he/she works to represent them.

5 A(n) .... is a rich and powerful businessman or industrialist.

6 A(n) .... is someone who has committed a crime or done something wrong.

7 A(n) .... is a person who helps another person to commit a crime.

8 A(n) .... is someone who is made to serve in one of the armed forces of a country whether he/she likes it or not.

9 A(n) .... is a noisy, rough young person who causes damage or disturbance in public places.

10 A(n) .... is a person responsible for keeping official records.

11 A(n) .... is a brother or a sister.

12 A(n) .... is a person who, during a strike, is placed outside a factory by his/her trade union to prevent other workers from going in until the strike is over.

13 A(n) .... is a foreigner who has not yet become a citizen of the country in which he/she is living.

14 A(n) .... is a skilled manual worker or craftsman.

15 A(n) .... is a young person who is in the care of a guardian or a law-court.

16 A(n) .... is someone who has withdrawn from society and lives alone.

17 A(n) .... is the former occupant of an office, position, etc.

18 A(n) .... is a person who makes insurance contracts.

19 A(n) .... is a person who holds that it is not possible to know whether God exists or not.

20 A(n) .... is a person in charge of a college or school who is responsible for the accounts.

21 A(n) .... is a person who writes the words for advertisements.

22 A(n) .... is a person of the same age, rank or status as oneself.

23 A(n) .... is a person who deceives others, usually to get money illegally.

24 A(n) .... is a person who is called in to settle a dispute between two people or groups – usually at the request of both sides.

25 A(n) .... is a fellow countryman or countrywoman.

26 A(n) .... is a ruler who uses his/her power unfairly or cruelly.

27 A(n) .... is a person who is entitled to receive money or property from a will or insurance policy.

28 A(n) .... is a small child who has just learnt to walk.

29 A(n) .... is a person whose job is to calculate the value of a property or the amount of income or taxes.

30 A(n) .... is a special messenger sent by one government to do business with another government.

Add two letters

Add **two letters** to each of the following words (in any place) to form a new word. A clue is given for each word to help you.

1 AGE .... keen
2 AID .... fast
3 ALE .... part of the body
4 BALE .... fighting
5 BARE .... a container for beer/liquids
6 BORE .... frontier
7 CAN .... expanse of water
8 CANE .... used to give light a long time ago
9 CARE .... not very plentiful
10 CASE .... a strongly built building used for defence
11 CATS .... a plant
12 COT .... shoreline
13 FEET .... a small furry animal
14 DOOR .... a profession
15 EAR .... very tired
16 FAIL .... one's parents, relatives, etc.
17 FEE .... an enclosure found around buildings, houses, etc.
18 GAP .... hold tightly
19 HEAT .... something money can't buy
20 LAY .... tall and thin
21 LEER .... intelligent, able to understand quickly
22 LICE .... a fish
23 LIE .... sheets, pillowcases, etc.
24 LUST .... an insect
25 MALE .... hard, often white, used for statues and buildings
26 NICE .... a metal
27 OUT .... a young person
28 PAD .... a gardening tool
29 PEA .... a form of musical entertainment
30 PEER .... often added to food

28

31	POLE	a breed of dog
32	RAIL	a country
33	RAM	found around paintings, windows and doors
34	RED	avarice
35	ROD	arrogant
36	ROW	a weapon, often used by American Indians
37	SEE	a vegetable
38	TALL	found in the theatre
39	WIT	another part of the body
40	WON	erroneous

Words that begin with "RE-"

Read through the clues/definitions and fill in the missing words, all of which begin with "re-".

1   a period of reduced trade, a slump or depression   `R E _ _ S S _ _`

2   someone who is **re**................... shows a lack of care about danger or about the results of his/her actions   `R E _ _ L _ _ S`

3   to scold someone officially and severely   `R E _ _ _ M _ _ D`

4   a place that provides protection   `R E _ _ G _`

5   to reward; to pay someone for work or trouble   `R E _ N _ _ T E`

6   a decision to stop doing something, e.g. to stop smoking. Often made on New Year's Eve   `R E _ _ L _ T _ _ N`

7   to echo   `R E _ E R _ _ R _ _ _`

8   an amount of money which is paid back to you because you have paid more tax, rent or rates than you needed to   `R E _ _ T _`

9   to move or slope backwards   `R E _ E _ E`

10   to get well again after an illness   `R E _ _ P _ R _ _`

11   if you **re**................... someone for something, you pay them back the money that they have spent   `R E _ M B _ _ _ _`

12   if you are **re**................... to do something, you are unwilling to do it   `R E _ _ _ T _ _ T`

13   people and things that are **re**................... are able to recover quickly from unpleasant or damaging events   `R E _ _ L _ _ N _`

14 to speak severely to someone because they have done or said something that you don't approve of

`R` `E` ` ` ` ` `K` ` `

15 a person who receives something

`R` `E` ` ` `I` ` ` ` ` ` ` `T`

16 someone who has recently joined an organisation or the army

`R` `E` ` ` `R` `U` ` ` ` `

17 to prove someone to be mistaken or a statement to be untrue

`R` `E` ` ` `U` ` ` ` `

18 a quick, rather angry, and often amusing answer

`R` `E` ` ` ` ` `R` ` `

19 to repeat the chief points of something that has been said

`R` `E` ` ` ` ` `P` ` ` `T` ` ` `L` ` ` ` ` ` `

20 if you **re**.................. something, you say that you will not accept it or have anything to do with it

`R` `E` ` ` ` ` `D` ` ` `T` ` `

21 if you are made **re**.................. , you are dismissed by your employer because there is not enough work

`R` `E` ` ` ` ` `N` `D` ` ` ` `

22 if you **re**.................. someone's feelings or behaviour towards you, you have the same feelings about them or behave the same way

`R` `E` ` ` `I` `P` ` ` ` ` ` ` `T` ` `

23 a container for keeping things in

`R` `E` ` ` `P` ` ` `C` `L` ` `

24 a part of a song that is repeated, especially at the end of each verse

`R` `E` ` ` ` ` `A` `I` ` `

25 a period of holiday between the sessions of work of a committee or parliament

`R` `E` ` ` ` ` `S` ` `

19 Words of similar meaning: Nouns

Complete each of the groups of three words with a word that is similar in meaning. Choose from the following:

adage	conjecture	profusion
adversary	dearth	turmoil
animosity	disdain	valour
apparel	feat	vow
brawl	flaw	woe
carcass	malady	wrath
clamour	prevarication	

1 abundance, plenty, copiousness ....
2 achievement, deed, exploit ....
3 lack, shortage, scarcity ....
4 anger, fury, rage ....
5 courage, daring, bravery ....
6 antagonism, hostility, enmity ....
7 assumption, supposition, presumption ....
8 blemish, fault, defect ....
9 body, corpse, cadaver ....
10 chaos, disorder, confusion ....
11 clothes, garments, attire ....
12 contempt, scorn, derision ....
13 enemy, antagonist, foe ....
14 fight, affray, mêlée ....
15 grief, sorrow, misery ....

16 illness, ailment, sickness ....

17 proverb, saying, maxim ....

18 lie, falsehood, fib ....

19 noise, tumult, uproar ....

20 oath, pledge, promise ....

20 Puzzle it out

Find two or three letters which will complete the first word and start the second. Fill in the spaces to make the second word. The clues will help you.

Example

a LI ☐O☐ ☐N☐ CE   King of the jungle/One time only

b SL ☐I☐ ☐M☐ AGE   Attractively thin/A picture formed in the mind

1 CEN ☐☐☐ ----   Middle part of something/A crime

2 APA ☐☐☐ --   Lack of interest, enthusiasm/Type of herb

3 AR ☐☐ ---   Particular space or surface/Used by an artist

4 CAT ☐☐ ---   Provide and serve food and drinks/Rub out

5 WA ☐☐ ---   What a surfer waits for/The poison that a snake injects into you when it bites

6 EARN ☐☐☐ ----   Serious and determined/The wide part of a river where it joins the sea

7 GO ☐☐ ---   A farm animal/A room at the top of a house

8 WAI ☐☐ ---   Part of the body/A way of looking

9 ID ☐☐ ---   Lazy, wasting time/Allowed by law

10 PR ☐☐ ---   Animal hunted and eaten by another animal/Where an eagle lives

11 SE ☐☐ ---   A sea creature/Permit

12 FOR ☐☐ ---   To make an illegal copy of something, e.g. a banknote/Birds, similar to ducks

13 BAR ☐☐☐ --   A container/An athletics track event

14 CAR ☐☐☐ --   Covers a floor/Part of a flower

15 DEN ☐☐ _ _ _ Thick and difficult to see through/To take possession by force

16 SPO ☐☐ _ _ _ An item of cutlery/A vegetable

17 TA ☐☐ _ _ Not wild/Not generous

18 PR ☐☐ _ _ _ A type of baby's cot on wheels/To make written changes in something, e.g. a law

19 LAP ☐☐ _ _ _ Part of a jacket/A sad poem or song usually about someone who has died

20 COA ☐☐ _ _ _ A vehicle/An unpleasant task

21 SPI ☐☐ _ _ _ _ Backbone/Used in sewing

22 OPA ☐☐☐ _ _ Cannot be seen through/A line of people

23 SI ☐☐ _ _ To write one's name/A small insect

24 BA ☐☐ _ _ Food put on a hook to catch fish/Makes you want to scratch

21 Confusing words

Choose the correct word in each of the following sentences:

1. Do you think the new tax changes will (affect/effect) you very much?

2. His behaviour at the party was (contemptuous/contemptible).

3. This must be the (definite/definitive) reference work on Roman history.

4. The doctor told him to use the (liniment/lineament) twice daily.

5. If you print that, I'll sue you for (libel/slander).

6. This is my last will and (testimony/testament).

7. We may have won all our matches this season, but we mustn't allow ourselves to become (complaisant/complacent).

8. I've always wanted to drive big (luxurious/luxuriant) cars.

9. The situation in China at the moment is tense and (volatile/voluble).

10. It is most (regretful/regrettable) that Mr Brown has decided to resign.

11. The police have (conclusive/decisive) proof that he robbed the bank.

12. How do you expect me to get the work finished when I'm (continually/continuously) being interrupted?

13. She was a very (intensive/intense) person, who seemed to care deeply about everyone and everything.

14. My father is a great believer in (alternate/alternative) medicine – especially homeopathy.

15. She had dyed her hair a (distinct/distinctive) shade of blue.

16. He spent three years in (goal/gaol) for embezzlement.

17. Do you enjoy (urban/urbane) life, or would you prefer to live in the country?

18. He was a man of (sanguine/sanguinary) temperament.

19. The Government are under no (illusions/delusions) about the difficulties facing the country.

20. My brother is (credible/credulous) enough to believe anything you tell him.

21. The Government are very worried about the (elicit/illicit) sales of champagne.

22. What can be (implied/inferred) from the Prime Minister's remarks?

23. I'm afraid the project is far too expensive to be (practical/practicable).

24. There was an (appreciative/appreciable) drop in temperature last night.

25. Tasmania lies in one of the (temperate/temporal) areas of the world.

26. Are these mushrooms (eatable/edible) or are they poisonous?

27. The majority of tinned food is (deficient/defective) in vitamins.

28 Only 25 per cent of people voted in the local election; the rest were completely (uninterested/disinterested).

29 The question of legal abortion is a very (emotional/emotive) issue in America.

30 The difference in performance between the two computers is (negligent/negligible).

31 The customs officer was very (official/officious) and made us open up all our bags.

32 There are very (strict/severe) laws in Sweden with regard to drinking and driving.

33 The company made (judicial/judicious) use of a Government grant.

34 Her performance was (masterful/masterly).

35 The caffeine in tea and coffee acts as a mild (stimulus/stimulant).

22 Same word – two meanings 1

Find the word which has two meanings in each of the following:

Example: a type of fish $\boxed{S|O|L|E}$ part of a shoe

1	found on a tree	☐☐☐☐	animal sound
2	part of a ship	☐☐☐☐☐	the top of the nose
3	behaviour	☐☐☐☐☐☐☐	to lead an orchestra
4	not clear	☐☐☐☐☐	lose consciousness
5	unspecific	☐☐☐☐☐☐☐	military officer
6	having no legal force	☐☐☐☐☐☐	a sick person
7	to go away	☐☐☐☐☐	permission to be absent from the army
8	a dark tar-like substance	☐☐☐☐	the highness or lowness of a musical note
9	to stagger	☐☐☐☐	a type of dance
10	a slow, dragging walk	☐☐☐☐☐☐	you do this when you play cards
11	a type of flower	☐☐☐☐☐	the total supply of goods kept by a retailer
12	to tread heavily or noisily	☐☐☐☐☐	someone who has no settled home
13	a type of fish	☐☐☐☐☐	a deep voice
14	a garment	☐☐☐☐	a headland
15	part of the body	☐☐☐☐☐	a container
16	a large bird	☐☐☐☐☐	a machine for lifting things
17	a tool	☐☐☐☐☐☐	a military exercise

18	a tree trunk	☐☐☐	a ship's diary
19	serious	☐☐☐☐☐	found in a cemetery
20	an animal's skin	☐☐☐☐	to keep out of sight
21	very small	☐☐☐☐☐☐	a measurement of time
22	the left side of a ship	☐☐☐☐	an alcoholic drink
23	to say no	☐☐☐☐☐	rubbish, waste material
24	noise	☐☐☐☐☐	a broad stretch of water
25	to hit	☐☐☐☐☐☐	to stop work

Sort out the words   1

Below are 40 words arranged alphabetically. Try to place each word under the correct heading. (There should be 5 words under each.)

arson	dandelion	lovage	sage
basil	embezzlement	magpie	skip
beaker	foxglove	mallet	spatula
bradawl	fraud	marjoram	starling
budgie	funnel	perch	tarragon
caddy	grater	perjury	treason
carnation	haddock	plaice	trout
cod	jackdaw	pliers	trowel
cowslip	keg	poppy	whisk
crate	ladle	rake	wren

Flowers
....
....
....
....
....

Herbs
....
....
....
....
....

Fish
....
....
....
....
....

Kitchen utensils
....
....
....
....
....

Tools/Gardening equipment
....
....
....
....
....

Containers/Receptacles
....
....
....
....
....

Birds
....
....
....
....
....

Crimes
....
....
....
....
....

24 Phobias and manias

Match up the words with the definitions.

1 agoraphobia
2 agromania
3 anthomania
4 claustrophobia
5 cynophobia
6 dipsomania
7 gynophobia
8 hydrophobia
9 kleptomania
10 megalomania
11 monophobia
12 necrophobia
13 nyctophobia
14 pyromania
15 toxiphobia
16 xenophobia

a a fear of water
b a fear of being alone
c a crazy desire to start fires
d a fear and dislike of foreigners or strangers
e a fear of open spaces
f a craze for flowers
g a fear of corpses
h a fear of poisoning
i a craze to be alone
j a fear of confined spaces
k a fear of the dark
l a fear of women
m a fear of dogs
n a delusion that one is great or powerful
o a compulsion to steal
p an uncontrollable desire for alcohol

Write your answers here:

1	2	3	4	5	6	7	8	9	10	11	12	13	14	15	16

25 Proverbs crossword

Complete the following crossword. Each word is part of a well-known English proverb.

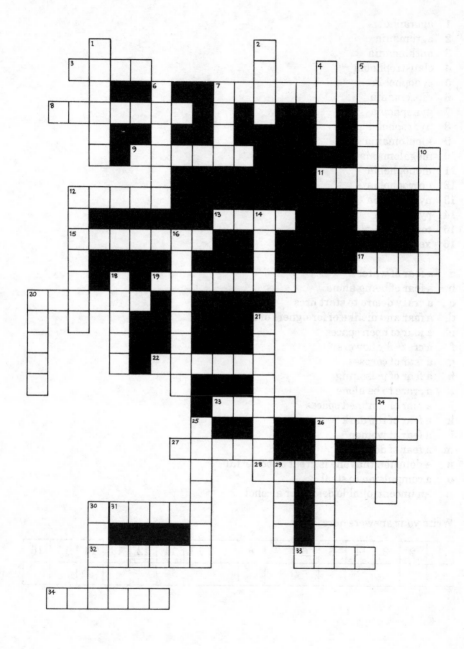

Across

3 A .... and his money are soon parted (4)
7 Don't make a mountain out of a .... (8)
8 The proof of the .... is in the eating (7)
9 First come, first .... (6)
11 A .... in time saves nine (6)
12 Every .... has a silver lining (5)
13 Don't put all your .... in one basket (4)
15 .... makes the heart grow fonder (7)
17 He who pays the piper calls the .... (4)
19 .... is the best policy (7)
20 Necessity is the .... of invention (6)
22 You can't teach an old dog new .... (6)
23 Out of the frying pan and into the .... (4)
26 .... waters run deep (5)
27 More .... , less speed (5)
28 One .... does not make a summer (7)
31 Too many cooks spoil the .... (5)
32 Nothing ventured, nothing .... (6)
33 Look before you .... (4)
34 Once .... , twice shy (6)

Down

1 Actions speak .... than words (6)
2 It's no use crying over spilt .... (4)
4 Where there's a .... there's a way (4)
5 Let .... dogs lie (8)
6 A friend in need is a friend .... (6)
7 A miss is as good as a .... (4)
10 Blood is .... than water (7)
12 .... begins at home (7)
14 Don't look a .... horse in the mouth (4)
16 Beggars can't be .... (8)
18 Two .... are better than one (5)
20 Great .... think alike (5)
21 One good turn .... another (8)
24 It's an ill wind that .... nobody any good (5)
25 Don't count your chickens before they are .... (7)
26 Speech is silver, ... is golden (7)
29 The early bird catches the .... (4)
30 Out of .... , out of mind (5)

26 Words that begin with "IN-"

Read through the clues/definitions and fill in the missing words, all of which begin with "in-".

1 to destroy unwanted things by burning

`I N _ _ N _ R _ T _`

2 people who are **in**.................... do not care how their behaviour affects other people

`I N _ _ N S _ D _ _ _ _ E`

3 a pain that you get when you find it difficult to digest food

`I N _ _ G _ S T _ _`

4 drunk

`I N _ B R _ _ _ D`

5 at the beginning; at first

`I N _ T _ _ _ Y`

6 to introduce a weak form of a disease into the body as a protection against the disease

`I N _ C _ L _ _ _`

7 not having money to pay what one owes

`I N _ _ _ V _ T _`

8 food or drink that is **in**.................... has very little taste

`I N _ _ P _ _`

9 if someone or something is **in**.................... they cannot be harmed or damaged

`I N _ L _ _ R _ B _ _`

10 to introduce someone important into a new place or job by holding a special ceremony

`I N _ _ G _ R _ _ _`

11 two things that are **in**.................... are unable to exist together because they are completely different

`I N _ _ _ P _ _ _ B _ _`

12 to charge someone formally with an offence in law

`I N _ _ _ T _`

13 to make someone very angry

`I N _ U _ _ _ T _`

14 an official inquiry to find out what caused someone's death

`I N _ _ _ S T`

15 someone who is **in**.................... is very rude and impolite

`I N _ _ L _ N _`

16 the introduction of a new idea, method or invention

I	N		V				N

17 something that is in.................. is absolutely essential

I	N			P		N	S			E

18 someone who is travelling in.................. is travelling in disguise or using another name so that he or she will not be recognised

I	N		G			O

19 that cannot be satisfied

I	N			T		B		

20 disbelief

I	N				D		L			Y

21 a substance that is burned for its sweet smell, often during a religious ceremony

I	N		E			E	

22 a narrow strip of water which goes from a sea or lake into the land

I	N			T

23 something that encourages you to do something

I	N			N		V	

24 an in.................. quality or ability is one which you are born with

I	N			T	

25 someone who is in.................. has faults or bad habits that will never change

I	N			R	R			B		E

27 Newspaper misprints 2

In each of the following extracts from a newspaper there is a misprint. Underline the word which is wrong and also write down which word should have been used instead.

Example: The 40-year-old man has dark hair with a prominent <u>fridge</u>. (..**fringe**..)

1 Red settee puppies ready now. Good pedigree. (..................)

2 There are three free weekends to be won. You'll get free fights, hotel rooms and spending money. (..................)

3 FOR SALE: Two pairs of vandals, nearly new. (..................)

4 Mr Davies walks with a limp and has a speed impediment. (..................)

5 George Keeping, 26, of Preston, has claimed all of Britain's 295 mountains. (..................)

6 The elderly couple in the top flat found the stars too much for them, so they sold it. (..................)

7 Councillor Black was a pretty officer in destroyers during the Second World War. (..................)

8 They have a full range of beers, wines and spirits and to complete the fayre, try one of their nasty bar snacks. (..................)

9 Watford police would like to trade two women who helped a driver after an accident. (..................)

10 The police arrived on the scene after a reported break-in and found a man writing in pain. (..................)

11 He said pickets in T-shirts and jeans had faced policemen with roses, riot shields, truncheons and dogs. (..................)

12 A cannabis smoker was discovered by his diluted eyes and furtive manner. (..................)

13 The price of the holiday includes all food, plus wind, coffee and cakes. (..................)

14 Mr and Mrs Webb left their only child at home while they went to the wedding of a fiend. (..................)

15 They say the land is in a conversation area and cannot be touched. (..................)

16 By using Prestel, customers will receive up-to-date information at the press of a bottom. (..................)

17 A television crew was in the studio to record the occasion for prosperity. (..................)

18 He was arrested and auctioned, but made no reply. He was then taken to West End Central police station. (..................)

19 Police and baliffs soon arrived, equipped with grappling irons and climbing bear. (..................)

20 He was stopped by the police who gave him a breast test. (..................)

28 Too many words 2

Replace the words in bold type in the following sentences with a single word. (The first letter of the word is given.)

1 The shop was offering a £5 **reduction from the full price** to any customer who paid in cash. (d...................)

2 After all the nuclear tests, the island was **not fit to live on**. (u...................)

3 We were all told of the decision **in advance**. (b...................)

4 The President has **absolutely and completely** refused to meet the terrorist leaders. (c...................)

5 We couldn't eat the food because it was **impure and likely to cause disease**. (c...................)

6 This ink is **impossible to rub out**. (i...................)

7 The two roads **cross each other** here. (i...................)

8 After months of negotiations, the treaty has now been **formally accepted**. (r...................)

9 All rooms must be **left empty** before 12 noon. (v...................)

10 Do you think the human race will be **completely destroyed** one day? (a...................)

11 The thieves got away with a large quantity of **gold and silver bars**. (b...................)

12 Plenty of fresh air and exercise is **likely to lead** to good health. (c...................)

13 The officer was **freed from blame** from the charges that had been made against him. (e...................)

14 He has a great **natural ability** for mathematics. (a...................)

15 His flat was **dirty and squalid**. (s...................)

16 I think you should change this sentence. As it stands now, it is **capable of more than one interpretation**. (a...................)

17 She was given an **annual allowance** of £3,000. (a...................)

18 Many people believe that a Third World War is **bound to happen**. (i...................)

19 The racing car **broke up into small pieces** as it hit the crash barrier at 300 m.p.h. (d...................)

20 The three men were arrested for **being on private land without permission**. (t...................)

Find someone

Look at the sentences below. Find someone:

who's turned over a new leaf	( )	who's doing time	( )
who's on leave	( )	who's named the day	( )
who's cheesed off	( )	who's at a loose end	( )
who's greasing someone's palm	( )	who's on the dole	( )
who's under someone's thumb	( )	who's pulling someone's leg	( )
		who's out of sorts	( )
who's got the chop	( )	who's for the high jump	( )
who's in arrears	( )	who's up in arms	( )
who's on tenterhooks	( )	who's blowing his/her own trumpet	( )
who's buttering someone up	( )		

a

MY WIFE IS THE BOSS IN OUR FAMILY. I DAREN'T DO ANYTHING WITHOUT ASKING HER FIRST.

b

I'VE BEEN OUT OF WORK FOR SIX MONTHS.

c

I REALLY MUST PROTEST! I THINK IT'S REALLY DISGRACEFUL THE WAY WE'VE BEEN TREATED!

d

I DON'T KNOW IF I'VE TOLD YOU THIS BEFORE, BUT I THINK YOU'VE GOT A WONDERFUL WAY WITH PEOPLE.

e

ONLY THREE MORE MONTHS OF MY SENTENCE TO GO.

f

I DON'T FEEL VERY WELL.

g

I'M GOING TO BE BETTER IN FUTURE. I PROMISE.

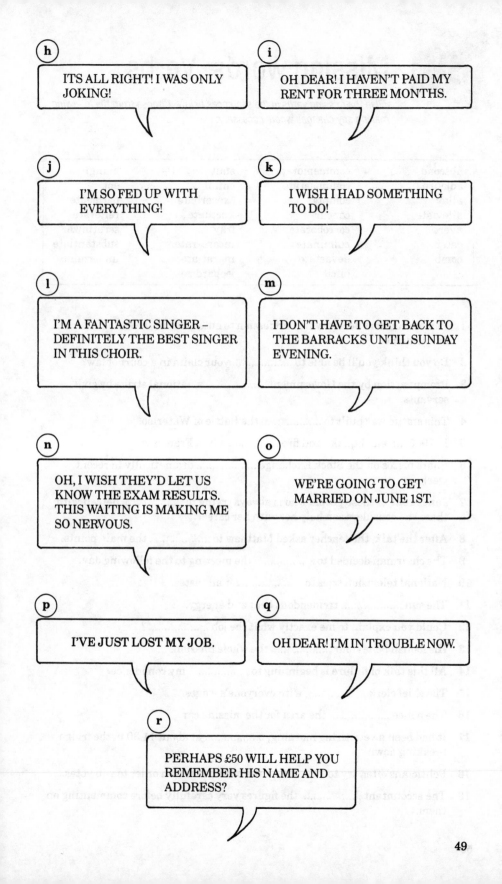

30 Missing words: Verbs

Fill in the missing verbs in the sentences below. Choose from the following, making any changes where necessary:

abscond	commemorate	emit	malign
adjourn	commiserate	entail	opt
allay	comply	exacerbate	permeate
alleviate	concur	fluctuate	reiterate
avert	corroborate	fray	scrutinize
cater	culminate	incarcerate	substantiate
comb	devastate	ingratiate	undermine
	elicit	jeopardize	

1 Pamela couldn't decide which profession to enter, but in the end .... for medicine.

2 Do you think you'll be able to .... your claim in a court of law?

3 Prompt action by the Government .... a national strike by civil servants.

4 This statue was built to .... the Battle of Waterloo.

5 In 1906, an earthquake and fire .... San Francisco.

6 Share prices on the Stock Exchange .... dramatically in recent weeks.

7 Jane is one of those people who is always trying to .... herself with those she considers can help her with her career.

8 After the talk, the teacher asked Matthew to .... the main points.

9 The chairman decided to .... the meeting to the following day.

10 National television tries to .... for all tastes.

11 The sun .... tremendous heat and energy.

12 Could you explain to me exactly what the job .... ?

13 His foolish behaviour .... the whole mission.

14 All this talk of failure is beginning to .... my confidence.

15 The chief clerk .... with everyone's wages.

16 The police .... the area for the missing car.

17 It had been a very tiring morning, ... at about 11.30 in the fridge breaking down.

18 Politicians often try to .... the other parties in order to win votes.

19 The accountant .... the figures very carefully before commenting on them.

50

20 Before the operation, the doctor tried very hard to .... the patient's fears.

21 All members are requested to .... with the club rules and regulations.

22 Tempers began to .... as the police tried to keep back the demonstrators.

23 The Prime Minister's action only managed to .... a situation that was already very serious.

24 The smell of tobacco smoke .... the whole house.

25 We did everything we could to .... the suffering of the wounded soldiers.

26 I .... with my friend over the loss of his sister.

27 Although we normally never see eye to eye, for once our opinions ....

28 The headmaster questioned each of the pupils in turn to try to .... the truth.

29 A passer-by .... the driver's account of the accident.

30 During the Second World War, Japanese people living in America .... (passive tense)

31 Homophones

A homophone is a word which sounds the same as another but is different in meaning or spelling. Below are 40 pairs of homophones. Look at the clues for each pair and try to work out what the words are. (Number 1 has been done for you.)

			Word a	*Word b*
1	a	it's all around us	**air**	**heir**
	b	will inherit one day		
2	a	used in snooker and billiards		
	b	a line of people		
3	a	to risk money to gain more money		
	b	to skip or jump about playfully		
4	a	a shade or tint of a colour		
	b	to cut with blows		
5	a	a round, flat piece of metal given as an award		
	b	to interfere		
6	a	two things or people		
	b	to cut away the outer covering of something with a sharp knife		
7	a	perfume		
	b	an American coin		
8	a	part of the body		
	b	to pull along behind with a rope		
9	a	just		
	b	the money paid for a journey		
10	a	the actors in a play		
	b	a social class		
11	a	harsh, rough		
	b	a series of education classes or medical treatment		
12	a	an implement for rowing		
	b	rock or earth from which metal can be obtained		
13	a	to put		
	b	a type of fish		
14	a	these appear when you cry		
	b	rows or levels placed one above the other		
15	a	a wild pig		
	b	a dull person		

16 a a percussion instrument
     b an emblem

17 a gold covering
     b a feeling that one is to blame for something
       or is at fault

18 a a disclosure of secret information
     b a vegetable

19 a a jetty
     b a member of the House of Lords

20 a a container for ashes
     b to receive money in return for working

21 a used by an artist
     b to solicit support or votes

22 a a number of notes played simultaneously
     b a thin rope or string

23 a candid
     b a French coin

24 a land surrounded by water
     b a corridor between two rows of seats (in a
       cinema, church, etc.)

25 a bodily suffering caused by injury or illness
     b a single sheet of glass

26 a not mistaken
     b a religious ceremony

27 a to move one's hand from side to side in
       greeting, farewell, etc.
     b to relinquish, give up, forgo

28 a a vegetable
     b a weight for jewellery

29 a part of an apple
     b a trained army group

30 a a manner of walking
     b used to close an opening in a wall, fence,
       field, etc.

31	**a**	part of a typewriter or piano	....
	b	landing place used for loading and unloading ships	
32	**a**	small opening found all over the skin	....
	b	to flow steadily and rapidly	
33	**a**	to summon to appear in court	....
	b	an area of ground for a building	
34	**a**	a sporting offence	....
	b	a domestic bird used as food	
35	**a**	stolen money or valuables	....
	b	a musical instrument	
36	**a**	to flatten buildings or towns	....
	b	to bring up (children)	
37	**a**	condensation found in the morning	....
	b	about to arrive	
38	**a**	to lose consciousness	....
	b	a mock attack or movement to distract an enemy or opponent	
39	**a**	a female horse	....
	b	the head of a city or borough	
40	**a**	a rough preliminary sketch	....
	b	a current of air	

32 Word bricks

Use 20 of the words on the bricks to complete the words at the bottom of the page.

ACT	AGE	AND	ART	BAN	CAP	CAT	CHIN	

	CON	EAR	EAT	ERA	GAG	GIN	HAM	HEAR

HER	INK	LET	LICE	NAG	ONE	PART	PIT	

	RID	TAR	TEN	TEST	THE	TOP	USE	VAN

1 EM.................LD

2 OC.................US

3 CA.................AL

4 H.................SE

5 AD.................CE

6 COR.................OR

7 RE.................SE

8 PR.................ICE

9 EN.................E

10 DISH.................ST

11 TRO.................RS

12 BR.................HE

13 MA.................ER

14 TR.................DY

15 C.................BER

16 CO.................UT

17 EN.................EER

18 ES.................E

19 LEAT.................

20 C.................OON

33 Missing words: Types of people 2

Fill in the missing words in the definitions below. Choose from the following:

actuary	delinquent	oculist	squatter
adjudicator	executor	pallbearer	stalwart
bigot	expatriate	pathologist	taxidermist
boor	interloper	pawnbroker	teetotaller
charlatan	invigilator	prude	tyrant
conscientious objector	lackey	punter	vagrant
convalescent	magnate	recidivist	vandal
	misogynist	spouse	

1   A(n) .... is a young person who has broken the law.

2   A(n) .... is someone who supervises the people taking an examination, making sure they do not cheat.

3   A(n) .... is a doctor who specialises in treating eye defects or diseases.

4   A(n) .... is someone who is easily shocked by things relating to nudity or sex.

5   A(n) .... is a loyal, dependable and strong supporter of an organisation or political party.

6   A(n) .... is a person who deliberately damages or destroys public property or things belonging to other people, usually for no apparent reason.

7   A(n) .... is a person who advises insurance companies on how much to charge for insurance.

8   A(n) .... is a person who behaves in a coarse, bad-mannered way.

9   A(n) .... is someone who is living in a foreign country.

10   A(n) .... is a person who is very wealthy and powerful, especially in business or industry.

11   A(n) .... is someone who walks beside or helps to carry a coffin at a funeral.

12   A(n) .... is a person who bets money on horse races.

13   A(n) .... is a person who has no home or job and who lives by going from place to place, begging or stealing.

14   A(n) .... is a person who cleans, prepares and preserves the skins of animals and then stuffs and mounts them so that they look lifelike.

15   A(n) .... is a person who is appointed to act as a judge in a competition.

16 A(n) .... is someone who refuses to serve in the armed forces or fight in a war on moral or religious grounds.

17 A(n) .... is a person who enters a place when he/she has no right to be there.

18 A(n) .... is a person who hates women.

19 A(n) .... is someone who never drinks alcohol.

20 A(n) .... is a person who has strong and often unreasonable opinions, especially about religion, race or politics, and is intolerant of those who do not share his/her opinions or beliefs.

21 A(n) .... is the person who carries out the orders in a will.

22 A(n) .... is a doctor who examines a dead body to find out how the person died.

23 A(n) .... is one's husband or wife.

24 A(n) .... is a ruler who has absolute power and who rules cruelly and unjustly.

25 A(n) .... is someone who deceives others by pretending to have special skills or knowledge, especially about medicine, that he/she does not really possess.

26 A(n) .... is a person who follows another person's orders completely without ever questioning them.

27 A(n) .... is a person who will lend you money in return for an article you possess, e.g. a watch. He/She has the right to sell the article if the money is not repaid within a certain time.

28 A(n) .... is a person who enters and lives in unoccupied property without permission and without paying any rent.

29 A(n) .... is a person who is spending time getting well after an illness.

30 A(n) .... is a person who keeps going back to a life of crime even after being punished; in other words, an incurable criminal.

Words that begin with "EX-"

Read through the clues/definitions and fill in the missing words, all of which begin with "ex-".

1   to kill someone as a lawful punishment

`E X _ C _ _ E`

2   hopeful; pregnant

`E X _ _ _ T _ N _`

3   a new room or building that is added to an existing building

`E X _ _ _ S _ _ N`

4   if you **ex**.................. someone from a difficult situation, you free him/her from it

`E X _ R _ C _ _ _`

5   to make worse

`E X _ C _ _ B _ T _`

6   a tax that the government of a country puts on goods that are produced for sale in that country

`E X _ _ S _`

7   to free someone from blame

`E X _ N _ R _ _ _`

8   a brave, bold and successful deed

`E X _ L _ _ T`

9   someone who is **ex**.................. is full of energy, excitement and cheerfulness

`E X _ B _ R _ _ T`

10 to look closely at something

`E X _ M _ _ _`

11 to be very good at something

`E X _ _ L`

12 to dismiss officially from a school, college, etc.

`E X _ E _`

13 when you **ex**.................. a group of animals or people they are all killed

`E X _ _ R _ _ N _ T _`

14 to return someone who may be guilty of a crime, and who has escaped, to another country for trial

`E X _ _ A D _ _ E _`

15 to annoy or make very angry

`E X _ S P _ _ A _ _`

16 freed from duty, service, payment, etc.

`E X _ _ P _`

17 if you **ex**.................. someone to do something, you try very hard to persuade him or her to do it

`E X _ _ _ T`

18	to take away something owned by another, often for public use	`E X _ R _ P _ I _ _ _`
19	to praise someone very highly	`E X _ _ L _ _`
20	to uncover something under the earth by digging	`E X _ _ _ V _ T _ _`
21	to come to an end; to die	`E X _ _ R _`
22	your **ex**.................. are the outermost parts of your body, especially your hands and feet	`E X _ R _ _ _ T _ _ S`
23	to leave out or shut out	`E X _ L _ _ E _`
24	a short piece of writing or music which is taken from a larger piece	`E X _ _ R _ T _`
25	to take a body out of the ground where it is buried	`E X _ U _ _`

35 Phrasal verbs 1

Complete each of the following sentences with a suitable verb (in the first part of the sentence) and a suitable preposition/particle (in the second part of the sentence).

Example:

I'd .....**give**..... up smoking, only I'm afraid of putting ......**on**....... weight.

1 When she was told that her father had .... away she broke ....

2 The police were .... in to break .... the fight outside the dance hall.

3 My father was .... up two days after war broke ....

4 She's .... out! Quick somebody! Get the smelling salts! That should bring her ....

5 Unless the group .... up soon we'll have to call .... the concert.

6 James .... into quite a large sum of money when his parents were killed when the plane they were in crashed as it was taking ....

7 I .... across these old books while I was clearing .... the attic.

8 "You will .... me up at the meeting, won't you, Bill?"
"Of course, Pat. You know you can count .... me for support."

9 I'm a bit .... up at the moment, Miss Brown. So perhaps you wouldn't mind dealing .... this matter instead.

10 Although there was a public outcry when the news .... out that the Prime Minister had been taking bribes, it didn't take long for all the fuss to die ....

11 What do you mean, you've .... out of cigarettes? I bought you two packets yesterday. You can't possibly have got .... them yet!

12 It took John a long time to .... over Cathy. In fact, it wasn't until he heard that she'd got married that he finally gave .... all hope of her ever going back to him.

13 If your son .... on working like this, Mrs South, then he's bound to get .... the exam in the summer.

14 I think I'd better .... in now; we're setting .... very early in the morning.

15 "Do you .... like dancing?"
"Well, I'd rather sit this one .... , if you don't mind."

16 Could you .... off another fifty copies of the letter please, Mr Wilson, and make sure they're sent .... first thing in the morning.

17 Things were really .... me down last week. In fact, I was almost tempted to do .... myself.

18 I don't know how I'd .... by if I didn't have my savings to fall ....

19 I've got some friends .... round this evening, so I'd better go home and tidy .... the flat before they arrive.

20 My daughter really .... on well with people. She takes .... her father in that respect.

Similes

Complete each of the similes below with a suitable word or words. Choose from the following:

a beetroot	an eel	a mule	putty
a bone	a flash	old boots	rain
a button	houses	an owl	a rake
the day is long	a judge	a peacock	a sheet
ditchwater	a kitten	pie	thieves
a dog	a lamb	pitch	velvet
a drowned rat	a lion	a poker	the weather
	a mouse	Punch	

1   as brave as ....

2   as bright as ....

3   as changeable as ....

4   as dark as ....

5   as dry as ....

6   as dull as ....

7   as easy as ....

8   as gentle as ....

9   as happy as ....

10 as pleased as ....

11 as proud as ....

12 as quick as ....

13 as quiet as ....

14 as red as ....

15 as right as ....

16 as safe as ....

17 as sick as ....

18 as slippery as ....

19 as smooth as ....

20 as sober as ....

21 as soft as ....

22 as stiff as ....

23 as stubborn as ....

24 as thick as ....

25 as thin as ....

26 as tough as ....

27 as weak as ....

28 as wet as ....

29 as white as ....

30 as wise as ....

37 Text: one word only

*Fill in the blanks in the following passage. Use **one word** only for each blank.*

I'm just beginning to .... (1) up to the fact that I'm no longer as young as I used to be. Of course, I'd .... (2) for some time that my birthday seemed to come .... (3) rather quickly and that I'd put on quite a bit of .... (4) – especially around the waist. But I didn't really think these things were .... (5) with age – I simply put them down to the increased pace of life plus .... (6) of exercise. In fact, I was .... (7) that I could still easily pass for thirty-four or thirty-five – it was just a question of .... (8) in my stomach and wearing the right sort of clothes. After all, I'd been brought up a firm believer in the .... (9) "You're as old as you feel" and as far as I was .... (10) I didn't feel a day over thirty.

So it came as quite a shock the other day when, just as I'd got on a bus on my way home from work, a young lady .... (11) me her seat. I mean, I could understand her giving up her seat to an old-age pensioner, but why me? Unless ... No, I .... (12) to believe the other alternative.

"It's all right, thank you. I'm getting off soon," I replied, forcing a smile, at the same time trying hard to convince myself that her .... (13) was some sort of protest for "Women's Lib". All the same, it took me a few days to get over the incident and I found myself continually scrutinizing my face in mirrors, trying hard to convince myself that the wrinkles around my eyes and on my forehead were not that .... (14) – not from a distance, anyway. My wife was very sympathetic and kept on trying to .... (15) my ego with such encouraging remarks as: "Of course you're not old, darling. You don't look a day over forty. Besides, grey hair makes you look distinguished."

That weekend, in a desperate .... (16) to persuade myself that there was still lots of .... (17) left in me yet, I .... (18) my wife into going to the dance hall we used to go to just before we got married. Unfortunately, the last time we had been there was more than twenty years ago, so I didn't find out until it was too late – until we were .... (19) inside the place – that it had been .... (20) into a discotheque. There couldn't have been anyone there over the age of twenty! To say that we stood out would be something of an .... (21). As for fox-trotting to blaring rock music, well, that was quite out of the .... (22). So we left rather quickly and spent the evening in the local pub instead.

I went to sleep that night feeling older and more depressed than .... (23).

38 Missing words: Nouns

Fill in the missing nouns in the sentences below. Choose from the following:

adage	conscription	fissure	prerequisite
anachronism	correlation	gist	prevalence
antidote	counterpart	heyday	quandary
backlog	deviation	idiosyncrasy	referendum
clemency	discrepancy	infringement	slick
coincidence	effigy	obituary	subsidy
compunction	euphemism	oversight	truancy
	figurehead	plaque	

1 When she returned from holiday, there was a(n) .... of work waiting for her.

2 The T.U.C. is the British .... of the Swedish L.O.

3 You told me you paid £2,000 for your computer, yet the bill only comes to £1,250. How do you explain the .... ?

4 "To pass away" is a(n) .... for "to die".

5 "Swinging London" was in its .... in the 1960s.

6 My uncle reads the .... column in *The Times* every morning just to check that he's still alive.

7 A(n) .... was held to determine the wishes of the people regarding nuclear power.

8 ".................. is a very small problem here," said the headmistress proudly. "Very few of our pupils don't enjoy coming to school."

9 "Spare the rod and spoil the child" is an old ....

10 It was such a(n) .... when I met my neighbour in Paris. I thought he was still at home.

11 No one doubts nowadays that there is a strong .... between smoking and lung cancer.

12 A large .... appeared in the playground just after the earthquake.

13 Having a job is in many ways a(n) .... to being able to enjoy and appreciate one's free time.

14 She was in a(n) .... as to whether to take the job or not. She just couldn't make up her mind.

15 In many ways sailing boats are a(n) .... in today's world of supersonic travel.

16 As it was his first offence, the magistrate showed .... and let him off with a warning.

17 Britain has a professional army, so .... is no longer needed.

18 I don't really have time to read this report now, Clare. Could you give me the .... of it?

19 Because of an unfortunate .... the complimentary tickets to the exhibition were not sent out until the day the exhibition closed.

20 There is a(n) .... of eye diseases in many tropical countries.

21 As far as I know there is no known .... for this poison.

22 She didn't have the slightest .... about phoning her boss and pretending she had a cold so that she could take the day off.

23 We must follow the plan to the letter; just the slightest .... could ruin everything.

24 Today's monarch has very little power; he or she is simply a(n) ....

25 According to this .... on the wall, Richard Burton was born here.

26 The National Opera in this country gets a Government .... of over £3,000,000 a year.

27 During the demonstration, some of the students burned a(n) .... of the Prime Minister.

28 The goal was disallowed because of a previous ....

29 There was an oil .... several miles long after the two oil tankers collided.

30 We all liked the new boss, but he did have one .... – he always wore a dandelion in his buttonhole.

39 Same word – two meanings 2

Find the word which has two meanings in each of the following:

Example: a type of fish $\boxed{S|O|L|E}$ part of a shoe

1	a small sum or amount	a dessert
2	an angry state of mind	to harden metal
3	progress	money lent or paid to somebody before the proper time
4	alter	money
5	agreement	to shrink
6	tendency	a religious dress
7	a metal	to show someone the way
8	to shape or form something	soft woolly growth found on bread, cheese, etc.
9	an insult	thin, frail
10	the part of a bride's dress that trails on the floor behind her	to instruct
11	a measurement	an enclosed area next to a building
12	to come near	surroundings
13	a sore on one's body	a cooking process
14	to talk to someone	opposite, contrary
15	to state clearly	to travel, or send something quickly

16	to make angry	☐☐☐☐☐☐☐	smoke of sweet-smelling spice
17	a journey by air or sea	☐☐☐☐☐☐☐	a brief section of a work of music or literature
18	a boulder	☐☐☐☐	a hard sweet in the shape of a long stick (popular at seaside resorts)
19	to put into words	☐☐☐☐☐	a country
20	a committee	☐☐☐☐☐	to get on a ship, train or aircraft
21	attractiveness	☐☐☐☐☐	a spell
22	a military rank	☐☐☐☐☐☐☐	relating to the body
23	a quarrel	☐☐☐	a line of houses
24	to eat food quickly	☐☐☐☐	a type of lock
25	abandon	☐☐☐☐☐☐	wasteland

40 Multiple-choice 2

Choose the word or phrase which best completes each sentence.

1 The strong smell of garlic seemed to .... the whole flat.

    a pierce   **b** penetrate   **c** inhabit   **d** pervade

2 The chairman of the local council had a .... interest in the building of a new supermarket near the town square. He owned the land there.

    a guaranteed   **b** permanent   **c** vested   **d** self

3 When we eat chicken in our house, my wife always insists on having the .... nose.

    a sailor's   **b** cock's   **c** parson's   **d** fowl's

4 He apologised profusely, swearing never to do it again. But his wife refused to be .... As far as she was concerned, he had done it once too often.

    a persuaded   **b** forgiven   **c** consoled   **d** mollified

5 After five weeks, both parties in the strike agreed that it should be settled by ....

    a arbitration   **b** ballot   **c** adjudication   **d** tribunal

6 Don't rush me; I hate having to make .... decisions.

    a sharp   **b** curt   **c** prompt   **d** snap

7 The sea between Dover and Calais was so .... that most of the passengers were seasick.

    a heavy   **b** bumpy   **c** choppy   **d** gusty

8 People who .... their food often get indigestion.

    a bolt   **b** munch   **c** nibble   **d** stuff

9 I can either move to another department or look for another job. It's .... choice really.

    a nobody's   **b** Hobson's   **c** sod's   **d** Murphy's

10 Most people agreed that the recent trial was a complete .... of justice.

    a satire   **b** corruption   **c** travesty   **d** abortion

11 My cousin earns her living by .... old paintings.

    a renewing   **b** restoring   **c** reimbursing   **d** renovating

12 I'm not quite sure I understand completely. Could you be a bit more
.... ?

   a explicit   **b** punctilious   **c** distinct   **d** explanatory

13 I can never look down from a high building; I suffer from ....

   a amnesia   **b** hypertension   **c** vertigo   **d** egomania

14 Two days before her wedding, my sister held a .... party for her
female friends.

   a bitch   **b** hen   **c** cow   **d** bridal

15 Her only income being a small allowance, she lived a very .... life.

   a frugal   **b** mean   **c** sparing   **d** extravagant

16 There was .... at the cinema when someone shouted "Fire!"

   a commotion   **b** pandemonium   **c** histrionics   **d** turbulence

17 When we missed the last bus home, we had no choice but to take ....

   a Shanks's pony   **b** Donald's donkey   **c** to arms
   d to first footing

18 I do wish you'd stop making .... remarks all the time, David. No
one's amused. Don't you realise how serious the problem is?

   a insincere   **b** comic   **c** facetious   **d** catty

19 "He thought that a Third World War was eminent" is an example of
....

   a alliteration   **b** a spoonerism   **c** a malapropism   **d** a pun

20 If she had a .... of good taste she'd know that those two colours just
don't go together.

   a pinch   **b** hint   **c** granule   **d** modicum

21 The new boss is so arrogant that he is completely .... to all criticism.

   a impermeable   **b** impervious   **c** void   **d** resistant

22 Being a Roman Catholic priest, no one doubted his ....

   a rancour   **b** veracity   **c** mendacity   **d** virility

Complete each of the following sentences with a suitable phrasal verb.

1 He won't be able to .... that speed. (maintain)

2 Mr Watkins is .... with some sort of virus infection. (confined to his bed)

3 Ms Wilson is .... Mr Thompson while he's on holiday. (taking the place of/substituting for)

4 I don't see why you .... foreigners. (despise)

5 I'm sorry to .... , but you're wanted on the phone. (interrupt)

6 We must .... a date for the firm's Christmas party soon. (arrange/decide upon)

7 Can you .... me .... for the night? (give me a place to sleep)

8 It will cost at least £1,000 to .... the flat. (decorate)

9 Her husband treats her really badly. I don't know how she .... it. (tolerates)

10 Let's .... these silly rules. (abolish)

11 It is very expensive to .... a large house nowadays. (maintain/look after)

12 I will never trust her again. She has .... me .... so many times. (failed me/disappointed me)

13 All our plans .... because of my sudden illness. (came to nothing)

14 The number of spectators has .... considerably in the past year. (decreased)

15 I wish I knew what .... his attacks. (caused)

16 "I hope I haven't .... you .... ?"
   "No, not at all. I never go to bed before midnight." (prevented you from going to bed)

17 If it .... soon, we'll be able to have our picnic as planned. (becomes fine)

18 It was the first time they had .... since they got married. (quarrelled)

19 Since four of the committee were ill, they decided to .... the meeting until the following week. (postpone)

20 To some extent the high standard of living in Sweden .... the boring social life. (compensates for)

21 You'd better not eat that food; it's .... (gone bad)

22 Each of the runners was given a number, but they decided to ....
.... number 13 in case anyone was superstitious. (omit)

23 When do British schools ....? (close for the holidays)

24 Dinosaurs .... millions of years ago. (became extinct)

25 Since it was his first offence, he was .... (not
punished/allowed to go free)

Look at the completed crossword below. See if you can work out which word goes with which clue. Write 1 Down, 5 Across, etc., in front of each clue. (See Test 8.)

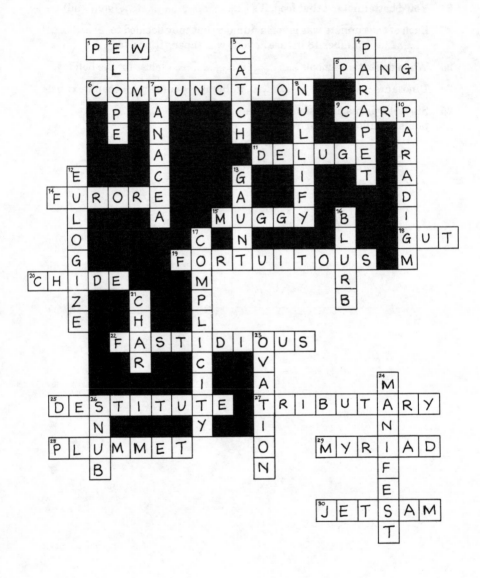

.... accidental, caused by chance

.... to fall violently straight down

.... a short promotional description of a book, printed on the cover or in advertisements

.... an awkward feeling of guilt, shame or remorse

.... a hidden problem or difficulty

.... to cause something to become black by burning

.... to scold, rebuke

.... thin and hungry-looking

.... a very angry or excited reaction by people to something

.... goods thrown overboard to make a ship lighter

.... to deliberately insult a person by ignoring him/her

.... a long, heavy rainfall usually causing flooding

.... something that is supposed to be a cure for any problem or illness

.... enthusiastic applause

.... completely without money or food, clothing, shelter etc.

.... a long wooden seat for members of a church or chapel congregation

.... warm and damp

.... to cancel, make void

.... to burn out or clear out the inside of a building

.... to commend, praise

.... a stream which flows into a river

.... a type of large freshwater fish that lives in rivers and lakes

.... a low wall along the edge of a roof, bridge or balcony

.... a sudden strong feeling, for example of pain or sadness

.... to run away secretly in order to get married – usually without one's parents' permission

.... the act of taking part with another person or persons in an illegal act or plan

.... easily disgusted, excessively difficult to please

.... a model or ideal

.... countless, innumerable

.... a list of goods carried on a ship

43 Idiomatic phrases

Complete the idiomatic phrases in the sentences below with a suitable word. Choose from the following:

bone	dead	French	pitch
casting	dirt	hush	splitting
chain	Dutch	inside	soft
close	flat	marked	sore
confirmed	foregone	open	stone

1 He's a .... smoker. No sooner has he stubbed out one cigarette than he lights another.

2 He said he had won it on the football pools, but we all knew it was .... money. He'd been given it to make sure he wouldn't go to the police.

3 Put the light on somebody! It's .... dark in here!

4 I think I'll go and lie down for a while; I've got a(n) .... headache.

5 The runners crossed the finishing-line at the same time. It was a .... heat.

6 He knew that once he had betrayed the I.R.A. he would be a .... man.

7 At the meeting, the voting was five for and five against, which meant the chairman had the .... vote.

8 He was so nervous about flying that he drank a large glass of whisky to give himself some .... courage.

9 The robbery went off so smoothly that the police suspected it was a(n) .... job.

10 This dress was .... cheap. It only cost £15.

11 My grandmother can't hear a thing. She's .... deaf.

12 Football has been a(n) .... point with him ever since he was dropped from the team.

13 I don't think Matthew will ever get married. He's a(n) .... bachelor.

14 They were bound to lose the election. It was a(n) .... conclusion.

15 It's no good coming to me for money, I'm .... broke.

16 We had a(n) .... shave the other day. A car almost hit us as we were crossing the road.

17 Her husband never lifts a finger in the house – he's .... idle.

18 It's a(n) .... secret that the new boss is gay.

19 He was so desperate to get home at the weekend to see his girlfriend that he decided to take .... leave.

20 I'm not surprised he married Maria. He's always had a(n) .... spot for Italians.

44 Words that begin with "CR-"

Read through the clues/definitions and fill in the missing words, all of which begin with "cr-".

1 a person or firm you owe money to

`C` `R` ` ` `D` ` ` `T` ` ` ` `

2 to burn a dead body at a special funeral ceremony

`C` `R` ` ` `M` ` ` ` ` `E`

3 an outdoor summer game

`C` `R` ` ` ` ` `U` ` ` `T`

4 something that is **cr**.................. is extremely important

`C` `R` ` ` ` ` `A` `L`

5 the study of secret writing and codes

`C` `R` ` ` `P` `T` ` ` ` ` ` ` `H` `Y`

6 a small box-shaped bed for a baby

`C` `R` ` ` `L` ` `

7 part of the skull

`C` `R` ` ` `N` ` ` `M`

8 deserving praise, honour, approval, etc.

`C` `R` ` ` `D` ` ` `T` ` ` ` ` `E`

9 a narrow crack or gap in a rock

`C` `R` ` ` `V` ` ` ` `

10 a sea voyage for pleasure

`C` `R` ` ` ` ` `S` ` `

11 a standard by which you judge something

`C` `R` ` ` `T` ` ` `R` ` ` ` `

12 to copy something that someone has written and pretend that it is your own work

`C` `R` ` ` ` `

13 severe pain by the sudden tightening of a muscle

`C` `R` ` ` `M` ` `

14 a very strong desire for something

`C` `R` ` ` `V` ` ` ` `

15 a letter or certificate that proves your identity or qualifications

`C` `R` ` ` `D` ` ` `N` ` ` ` ` `L` ` `

16 an underground room beneath a church or cathedral

`C` `R` ` ` ` ` `T` ` `

17 the plates, cups and saucers that you use at mealtimes

`C` `R` ` ` `C` ` ` ` ` `Y`

18	stupid, insensitive, unfeeling	C	R			S		

18 stupid, insensitive, unfeeling 　C R ☐ ☐ S

19 if you are **cr**.................. , you are always ready to believe what people tell you, and are easily deceived 　C R ☐ D ☐ L ☐ ☐

20 to lower the body close to the ground by bending the knees and back 　C R ☐ ☐ C ☐

21 a type of shellfish 　C R ☐ ☐ F ☐ ☐ H

22 a musical note 　C R ☐ ☐ C ☐ T

23 something worn by men 　C R ☐ A ☐

24 a person with very strange, odd or peculiar ideas 　C R ☐ N ☐

25 a very popular fashion, usually for a short time 　C R ☐ ☐ E ☐

45 Missing words: Types of people 3

Fill in the missing words in the definitions below. Choose from the following:

big shot	fence	mole	soft touch
brick	gate-crasher	old maid	sponger
busybody	grass	rough diamond	swot
chatterbox	grass widow	scab	tout
dab hand	guinea pig	skinflint	underdog
dark horse	kerb crawler	slavedriver	wet blanket
diehard	lame duck	smart aleck	whizz kid
dogsbody	landlubber		

1 A(n) .... is a woman whose husband is away for a period of time.

2 A(n) .... is a person who is not used to the sea or ships.

3 A(n) .... is someone who continues to work when his/her fellow-workers are on strike.

4 A(n) .... is a person who dislikes spending or giving money.

5 A(n) .... is a person who offers tickets that are in short supply for sale for a price higher than usual.

6 A(n) .... is a very important or influential person.

7 A(n) .... is someone who cannot stop talking.

8 A(n) .... is a person who turns up at parties without being invited to them.

9 A(n) .... is a person who works inside an organisation for a long time in order to provide secret information for the enemy.

10 A(n) .... is a person who annoys others by claiming to know everything and trying to sound clever.

11 A(n) .... is a person from whom it is easy to get what one wants, for example money, because he/she is kind or easily deceived.

12 A(n) .... is a person with modern ideas who works with energy and enthusiasm and achieves great success in his or her job while still young.

13 A(n) .... is a very nice, dependable person.

14 A(n) .... is a person who buys and sells stolen goods.

15 A(n) .... is someone in a low-ranking position who has to do all the boring jobs that no one else wants to do.

16 A(n) .... is a person with a kind and generous nature, but whose outward appearance or manner is rather rough.

17 A(n) .... is a person who is expected to lose in a competition with someone else, or a weaker person who is always treated badly by others.

18 A(n) .... is a person who is very inquisitive about other people's affairs.

19 A(n) .... is a person who has greater capabilities than he/she shows or than people are aware of.

20 A(n) .... is someone who informs the police about the people concerned in a crime. This person is often a criminal himself/herself.

21 A(n) .... is a person who is weak or a failure in some way and has to be helped by others.

22 A(n) .... is a woman who is unlikely ever to get married.

23 A(n) .... is someone who makes people work very hard.

24 A(n) .... is someone who studies very hard especially when trying to get good examination results.

25 A(n) .... is a person who is very good at something.

26 A(n) .... is a person who is used as a subject in medical or other experiments.

27 A(n) .... is a person who is always taking money and things off other people, usually by taking advantage of their generosity or weakness.

28 A(n) .... is a person who discourages or prevents others from enjoying themselves by being boring and negative towards everything.

29 A(n) .... is someone who refuses to change his/her ideas and opinions (usually political ones).

30 A(n) .... is a man who annoys women by following them slowly in a car when they are walking along the street.

46 From Part to Gain

Change the word PART into GAIN in twenty-five moves, changing one letter at a time. Some letters have been added to help you.

	P	A	R	T	
1					having a sharp taste, sour
2					the weight of an unloaded goods vehicle
3					without clothes
4	B				to make a hole in something
5					part of an apple
6					grown in fields
7					pulled violently apart or into pieces
8					the name of one of the British political parties
9					a wrongful but not criminal act that can be dealt with in a civil court of law
10					this person can usually get you tickets for any West End play or musical
11					a boxing match
12			T		to run away suddenly

13					something you wear
14					the skin of an animal with the hair still attached
15					can be used instead of coal
16	B				the regular path or route followed by a policeman on duty
17					a bad-mannered child (derogatory)
18					to boast
19					a steep, rugged mountain peak or rock
20	C				to revise intensively for an examination
21					used by babies
22					easily shocked by anything rude
23					unpleasant, not cheerful
24					a wide smile showing the teeth
	G	A	I	N	

47 Foreign words and phrases

A lot of foreign words and phrases are used in English. See if you understand the following by putting each of them into one of the sentences below.

ad hoc	coup d'état	kudos	quid pro quo
ad infinitum	curriculum vitae	non compos mentis	rapport
alfresco	de facto	non sequitur	status quo
aplomb	détente	per capita	tête-à-tête
avant garde	ex officio	per se	vice versa
blasé	extra-curricular	persona non grata	vis-à-vis
bona fide	faux pas	post mortem	
carte blanche	in camera	prima facie	

1   The General overthrew the President and became the .... ruler of the country.

2   What is the average .... income in your country?

3   It says in the invitation that wives are allowed to bring their husbands and .... So I shall certainly take Anne with me.

4   If you ask me, most of this .... music is rubbish. Give me Beethoven or Mozart any day!

5   You made a terrible .... when you asked how his wife was. Didn't you know that she'd recently run off with his best friend?

6   They decided to set up an .... committee to deal with the urgent problem that had come up.

7   He was thrown out of the country two years ago and has been .... since then.

8   Generally speaking, students are against preserving the .... in a country. They usually want change and reform.

9   She gained a lot of .... after her third successful novel.

10   He came to power in a violent and bloody ....

11   As President she will be a(n) .... member of several important committees.

12   The car park is for .... customers only. No one else is allowed to use it.

13   As there seems to be a .... case against him, they decided to press for a trial immediately.

14   When Ronald Reagan and Margaret Thatcher met for the first time, there was an instant .... between them.

15 Don't mention golf when Charles is around; otherwise he'll go on .... about it.

16 It is hard to believe in the present .... that the two countries were at war with one another less than two years ago.

17 The Prime Minister handled the hostile questioning of the journalists with great ....

18 Your argument is a .... and totally irrelevant!

19 I'd like to see you tomorrow, John, ... the proposed new changes. I'd just like to hear what you think of them.

20 It was a very nice house .... , but it wasn't quite the sort of place we were looking for.

21 The case involved discussing matters which were top secret, so it was held ....

22 No one told me what to do. I was given .... to organise things as I saw fit.

23 Aᵣ plicants must send in a full .... no later than Friday, March 24th.

24 ᴡe usually eat .... in the summer.

?ᴊ He gave me a 10 per cent discount as a .... for having helped him mend his car.

26 He was believed to have been .... when he attempted to commit suicide.

27 Visiting Russia so often has made him very .... about eating caviar.

28 Our school offers a wide range of .... activities, including photography, karate and folk-dancing.

29 I had a very interesting .... with the new manager last week. Now I think I understand what he plans to do.

30 The .... examination showed that she had died of a heart attack.

48 Choose the answer

Choose the correct answer for each of the following:

1 The words low, udder, heifer and Jersey all have something to do with:

   a rowing   **b** cows   **c** houses   **d** weapons   **e** fishing

2 Who would take the Hippocratic oath?

   a a barrister   **b** a soldier   **c** a zoo keeper   **d** a priest
   e a doctor

3 Which of the following is incorrect?

   a a clod of earth   **b** a sliver of glass   **c** a wad of cotton
   d a clump of grass   **e** a segment of orange

4 Who would use a score?

   a a policeman   **b** a surgeon   **c** a hairdresser
   d a tennis umpire   **e** a conductor

5 Which phrase is the 'odd one out'?

   a to kick the bucket   **b** to bite the dust   **c** to touch wood
   d to pass away   **e** to croak

6 This part is called:

   a a rung
   b a plank
   c a foothold
   d a wedge
   e a crossbar

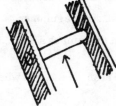

7 To be "indomitable" is to be:

   a faultless   **b** stubborn, unyielding   **c** bossy, domineering
   d disobedient, rebellious   **e** persevering, full of stamina

8 What does a dasymeter measure?

   a altitude   **b** wind speeds   **c** rainfall   **d** the potency of drugs
   e the density of gases

9 A dog barks. Which animal gobbles?

   a a frog   **b** a turkey   **c** a hyena   **d** a crow   **e** an owl

10 Complete this proverb. "Time and tide . . ."

   a are soon parted   **b** wait for no man
   c makes the heart grow fonder   **d** knows no end   **e** has no return

11 If you were suffering from phlebitis, you would have trouble with your:

a joints   **b** veins   **c** nerves   **d** mouth   **e** skin

12 Which of the following ways of walking would you associate with someone who had drunk too much alcohol?

a stagger   **b** swagger   **c** plod   **d** tramp   **e** prowl

13 Which of these is *not* part of a house?

a a loft   **b** a skylight   **c** a porch   **d** French windows
e a postbox

14 If you were suffering from scopophobia, you would hate:

a being stared at   **b** being alone   **c** cats   **d** going in lifts
e bright lights

15 What is the following?

a a press stud
b a toggle
c a clasp
d a Welsh button
e a hook and eye

16 Complete the following: "Scuttle, coffer, carton ..."

a milk   **b** lathe   **c** hoe   **d** clutch   **e** urn

17 Which of the following is *not* a fish?

a halibut   **b** mackerel   **c** gannet   **d** haddock   **e** skate

18 Who would use a hod?

a a shoemaker   **b** a nurse   **c** a bricklayer   **d** a pilot
e a carpenter

19 Complete the following phrase. "He fell for the story hook, line and ..."

a liver   **b** quartered   **c** sinker   **d** fish tank   **e** everywhere

20 Where would you wear galoshes?

a on your hands   **b** under your shirt   **c** on your head
d over your shoes   **e** around your waist

49 Sort out the words 2

Below are 40 words arranged alphabetically. Try to place each word under the correct heading. (There should be 5 words under each.)

abhor	choker	haul	saunter
abominate	chuckle	hernia	shingles
amble	clasp	hobble	smirk
beam	despise	hoot	smock
beret	earwig	loathe	snigger
bray	execrate	louse	strut
catarrh	flip-flop	lug	tow
caw	gnat	midge	trudge
centipede	gout	muffler	whinny
chirp	guffaw	mumps	wrench

Clothes and accessories
....
....
....
....
....

Diseases/illnesses
....
....
....
....
....

Insects
....
....
....
....
....

Animal sounds
....
....
....
....
....

Expressing dislike/ hatred
....
....
....
....
....

Smiling and laughing
....
....
....
....
....

Taking, holding and pulling
....
....
....
....
....

Ways of walking
....
....
....
....
....

Matching pairs

a Toxicology is the study of poisons. What about the following?
Match them up.

1 anthropology ...
2 entomology ...
3 ethnology ...
4 etymology ...
5 graphology ...
6 meteorology ...
7 odontology ...
8 ornithology ...
9 palaeontology ...
10 philology ...

a the study of teeth
b the study of birds
c the study of the origin of words
d the study of fossils
e the study of man as an animal
f the study of insects
g the study of language
h the study of weather and climate
i the study of different races and their relationships
j the study of handwriting

b A feminist is one who believes in equal rights for women.
What about the following? Match them up.

1 accompanist ...
2 arborist ...
3 arsonist ...
4 somnambulist ...
5 genealogist ...
6 sadist ...
7 lepidopterist ...
8 lexicologist ...
9 masochist ...
10 numismatist ...

a one who sets fire to property
b one who studies the history and meaning of words
c one who plays an instrument in support of a singer
d one who traces the history of families
e one who walks in his/her sleep
f one who studies trees
g one who studies butterflies and moths
h one who gets pleasure from being cruel to others
i one who studies and collects coins
j one who gets gratification in suffering pain

c Match up each of the words on the left with a word on the
   right to form completely new words.

1	back	loose
2	bed	gap
3	court	fall
4	fire	sight
5	foot	strong
6	head	biting
7	man	ship
8	over	arm
9	stop	hole
10	wind	rock

d What sound does water or broken glass make? Complete the
   following by choosing an appropriate word from those on the
   right.

1	the .... of coins	blast
2	the .... of hoofs	clank
3	the .... of a rifle	clatter
4	the .... of an explosion	creak
5	the .... of tiny feet	jingle
6	the .... of a hinge	lapping
7	the .... of leaves	patter
8	the .... of heavy chains	report
9	the .... of broken glass	rustling
10	the .... of water	tinkle

e   Complete each of the phrases on the left with a suitable adjective. Choose from the words on the right. Use each adjective once only.

1	a(n) .... accident	decisive
2	a(n) .... escape	fragrant
3	a(n) .... account	impenetrable
4	a(n) .... reader	tricky
5	a(n) .... battle	fatal
6	a(n) .... problem	ambiguous
7	a(n) .... smell	lucky
8	a(n) .... plan	vivid
9	a(n) .... statement	avid
10	a(n) .... jungle	ingenious

f   "Baldness" is a more everyday word for "alopecia". What about the following? Match them up.

1	arteriosclerosis ...	a.	piles
2	bursitis ...	b.	the change of life
3	cerebral haemorrhage ...	c.	lockjaw
4	convulsions ...	d.	housemaid's knee
5	coronary thrombosis ...	e.	indigestion
6	contusion ...	f.	German measles
7	dyspepsia ...	g.	hardening of the
8	haemorrhoids ...		arteries
9	halitosis ...	h.	fits
10	hernia ...	i.	short-sight
11	hydrophobia ...	j.	bruise
12	menopause ...	k.	wind
13	myopia ...	l.	rabies
14	rubella ...	m.	bad breath
15	tetanus ...	n.	heart attack
16	flatulence ...	o.	rupture
		p.	stroke

Answers

TEST 1

1	irate	8	frugal	15	stingy
2	belligerent	9	obese	16	destitute
3	valiant	10	clamorous	17	copious
4	cumbersome	11	impetuous	18	opulent
5	wily	12	ravenous	19	coy
6	perilous	13	discrepant	20	paltry
7	fervent	14	slothful		

TEST 2

1	feat	13	collection	25	item
2	pride	14	quiver	26	stretch
3	series	15	joint	27	clump
4	stroke	16	tuft	28	clap
5	troupe	17	shock	29	block
6	anthology	18	breath	30	state
7	course	19	grain	31	article
8	medley	20	plot	32	flash
9	rasher	21	speck	33	gaggle
10	spell	22	term	34	panel
11	wad	23	colony	35	roar
12	attack	24	school	36	plague

TEST 3

1	ambidextrous	8	adjourned	15	negligible
2	disembarked	9	cowardice	16	devastated/destroyed
3	obsolete	10	exceeded	17	airworthy
4	Extensive	11	meanders	18	amnesia
5	adhesive	12	dentures	19	ascertain
6	armistice	13	impregnable	20	insatiable
7	jeopardized	14	matricide		

TEST 4

1	cursory	11	requisite	21	eligible
2	heinous	12	slushy	22	indicative
3	indigenous	13	vivid	23	prevailing
4	petty	14	avid	24	spontaneous
5	squeamish	15	dishevelled	25	commensurate
6	adamant	16	implicated	26	exorbitant
7	feasible	17	incessant	27	inopportune
8	implicit	18	sedentary	28	prolific
9	irrevocable	19	unanimous	29	congested
10	plausible	20	circumstantial	30	redundant

TEST 5

1	– 7	3	–	1
2	– 9	4	–	6

5	–	8	8	–	10
6	–	4	9	–	5
7	–	3	10	–	2

TEST 6

1	core	11	tooth	21	rung
2	relay	12	udder	22	kernel
3	spoke	13	umpire	23	hammer
4	cushion	14	lobe	24	pimp
5	jacket	15	gills	25	estuary
6	wick	16	stem	26	rafter
7	bonnet	17	wreath	27	funnel
8	flue	18	parting	28	cuff
9	pulpit	19	mane	29	handset
10	hand	20	lapel	30	bridge

TEST 7

1	draw	10	collect	18	call
2	follow	11	hold	19	drive
3	make	12	see	20	form
4	throw	13	bear	21	serve
5	acquire	14	cook	22	cut
6	drop	15	fill	23	keep
7	hang	16	play	24	lose
8	read	17	take	25	lead
9	alleviate				

TEST 8

1	Across	to search and steal
13	Across	to walk at an easy, gentle pace
8	Across	to steal in small amounts
12	Down	living both on land and in water
5	Across	learned, scholarly
25	Across	a two-hundredth anniversary
17	Across	an inscription on a tomb
27	Across	one of the signs of the Zodiac
27	Down	a loud whistle or cry expressing disapproval or displeasure at the theatre, a sports match, etc.
3	Down	to fall like a waterfall
16	Across	short-lived, lasting only a day or so
20	Across	talkative, wordy
14	Across	extremely overweight
7	Across	a task that is unpleasant or boring
24	Down	wreckage found floating on the surface of the sea
29	Across	a kind of chicory, used as salad
9	Across	to idle, loiter, waste time
4	Across	to defer, delay in doing some necessary act
2	Down	imprisoned, confined
15	Down	slightly hungry
21	Down	a natural sleep of some animals throughout the winter
22	Down	a word or sentence that reads the same backwards and forwards
10	Down	to listen secretly to a private conversation
11	Across	to separate by cutting

6	Down	prone to anger, irritable
18	Down	at the point of death, dying
19	Across	a list of prices and charges
28	Across	a type of small flying insect (like a mosquito) that bites people
23	Down	a sweet-smelling garden flower
26	Across	smuggled goods

TEST 9

1	d	acquitted	12	b	inhibited
2	a	lurking	13	d	obsolete
3	b	glare	14	a	scratch
4	a	enunciation	15	c	defer
5	b	invariably	16	a	done in
6	c	devoid	17	d	rudimentary
7	d	emaciated	18	a	tantamount
8	d	an expletive	19	b	divulge
9	c	overhaul	20	b	prerogative
10	a	cited	21	c	itinerary
11	c	gab	22	a	imperative

TEST 10

	Misprint		Correct word
1	bunk		bulk
2	rend		send
3	bomb		comb
4	sin		sun
5	bra		bar
6	tickle		tackle
7	bedpan		deadpan
8	death		health
9	suspicious		auspicious
10	germs		gems
11	boob		boom
12	lion		loin
13	thing		thigh
14	rub		rug
15	strangled		stranded
16	onion		union
17	gloves		cloves
18	cows		vows
19	prevented		presented
20	boar		board

TEST 11

1	abridge	8	dupe	15	chide
2	procure	9	corroborate	16	scurry
3	revere	10	coerce	17	jibe
4	vex	11	abhor	18	allure
5	bicker	12	snicker	19	fathom
6	postulate	13	thwart	20	pillage
7	crow	14	shelve		

TEST 12

1   True
2   True
3   False   (It means "last but one")
4   True   (It's a type of hat)
5   False   (A cantankerous person is very bad-tempered)
6   False   (It's a type of furry flower which grows on certain trees, e.g. birch, willow)
7   False   (It's very fine rain)
8   True
9   False   (It's a small, fierce animal of the weasel family)
10 True   (It's animal waste)
11 False   (It should be "I'm invisible!". "Invincible" means "too strong to be defeated".)
12 True
13 False   (A pervert is someone whose sexual behaviour is not considered natural)
14 False   (It means "every two years")
15 True   (Its full name is "budgerigar". It's a small brightly coloured bird. Some budgerigars can be taught to speak)
16 True   (It's a flat-bottomed boat, used for carrying heavy loads – especially on canals)
17 True
18 True   (It's a raised platform)
19 False   (If you have halitosis you have bad breath)
20 False   (It's the lowest point of something)
21 True   (They are the metal bars in a bicycle wheel)
22 False   (It is used to check the amount of oil in a car's engine)
23 True   (A chinwag is another word for a chat)
24 True
25 False   (A turf accountant is another name for a bookmaker – i.e. someone you go to to place bets on a horse race or a dog race)

TEST 13

1   stilted
2   stirrup
3   stuffy
4   strenuous
5   stagnant
6   starboard
7   stink
8   stupor
9   stalls
10 stalk
11 steamroller
12 stump
13 strident
14 statutory
15 stealthy
16 stockpile
17 stingy
18 stoop
19 stodgy
20 stance
21 stretcher
22 stilton
23 staid
24 starling
25 stocky

TEST 14

Joke 1

(1) Grandma was nearly ninety years of age when she won £375,000 on the football pools. Her family were extremely (2) worried about her heart and feared that the news of her large win would (3) come as too much of a shock for her.

"I think we had better (4) call in the doctor to tell her the news," suggested the eldest son.

The doctor soon arrived and the (5) situation was explained to him.

"Now, you don't have to worry about anything," said the doctor. "I am fully trained in such delicate matters and I feel sure I can (6) break this news to her gently. I assure you, there is absolutely no need for you to fear for her health. Everything will be quite (7) safe if left to me."

The doctor went in to see the old lady and gradually brought the conversation around to (8) football pools.

"Tell me," said the doctor, "what would you do if (9) you had a large win on the pools – say over three hundred and fifty thousand pounds?"

"Why," replied the old lady, "I'd (10) give half of it to you, of course."

The doctor fell down dead with shock.

Joke 2

(11) It was one of the strangest looking dogs they had ever seen at the pub, and the (12) regulars found it a great topic of conversation.

Eventually one of them sidled over to the dog's owner and said, (13) "That's a stupid looking dog you've got there. Can it fight?"

"Sure," (14) replied the owner.

"Well," said the man, "I bet you £10 that my labrador can beat your dog."

The owner (15) accepted the bet and the labrador was led in to fight. After twenty-five seconds the labrador lay (16) dead on the floor. The loser, looking down at his dead dog, shook his head sadly and said, "Your dog can certainly (17) fight. But I still think it's a funny looking dog."

"Yes," agreed the owner. "And it (18) looked even funnier until I shaved its mane off."

Joke 3

(19) The Englishman was in a restaurant in Scotland when he was suddenly attacked by a (20) severe burst of coughing and sneezing – and he sneezed so violently that his false teeth (21) flew out of his mouth and dropped to the floor, where they broke at the feet of the Scotsman.

"Don't worry, sir," (22) said the Scotsman. "My brother will soon get you a new pair and at far less cost than an English dentist would (23) charge. And he can provide a suitable set almost immediately."

The Englishman couldn't believe his luck and gladly (24) accepted the Scotsman's offer.

The Scotsman left the restaurant and returned ten minutes later with a pair of (25) false teeth which he handed to the Englishman.

"Fantastic!" exclaimed the Englishman, trying the teeth. "They (26) fit perfectly. Your brother must be a very clever dentist."

"Oh, he's (27) not a dentist," replied the Scotsman. "He's an undertaker."

TEST 15

1	onset	13	by-pass	25	outset
2	downpour	14	write-up	26	getaway
3	outcome	15	outbreak	27	downfall
4	takeaway	16	lookout	28	build-up
5	hold-up	17	breakup	29	turnout
6	output	18	setbacks	30	outburst
7	cover-up	19	tailback	31	turnover
8	drawbacks	20	outlay	32	outlook
9	cutbacks	21	breakthrough	33	intake
10	upbringing	22	checkup	34	outcry
11	write-off	23	comeback	35	lay-by
12	break-in	24	layout		

TEST 16

1	castaway	4	shop steward	7	accomplice
2	gossip	5	tycoon	8	conscript
3	midwife	6	culprit	9	hooligan

94

10 registrar	17 predecessor	24 arbitrator
11 sibling	18 underwriter	25 compatriot
12 picket	19 agnostic	26 despot
13 alien	20 bursar	27 beneficiary
14 artisan	21 copywriter	28 toddler
15 ward	22 peer	29 assessor
16 hermit	23 swindler	30 envoy

TEST 17

1 EAGER	15 WEARY	28 SPADE
2 RAPID	16 FAMILY	29 OPERA
3 ANKLE	17 FENCE	30 PEPPER
4 BATTLE	18 GRASP	31 POODLE
5 BARREL	19 HEALTH	32 BRAZIL
6 BORDER	20 LANKY	33 FRAME
7 OCEAN	21 CLEVER	34 GREED
8 CANDLE	22 PLAICE	35 PROUD
9 SCARCE	23 LINEN	36 ARROW
10 CASTLE	24 LOCUST	37 SWEDE
11 CACTUS	25 MARBLE	38 STALLS
12 COAST	26 NICKEL	39 WAIST
13 FERRET	27 YOUTH	40 WRONG
14 DOCTOR		

TEST 18

1 recession	10 recuperate	18 retort
2 reckless	11 reimburse	19 recapitulate
3 reprimand	12 reluctant	20 repudiate
4 refuge	13 resilient	21 redundant
5 remunerate	14 rebuke	22 reciprocate
6 resolution	15 recipient	23 receptacle
7 reverberate	16 recruit	24 refrain
8 rebate	17 refute	25 recess
9 recede		

TEST 19

1 profusion	8 flaw	15 woe
2 feat	9 carcass	16 malady
3 dearth	10 turmoil	17 adage
4 wrath	11 apparel	18 prevarication
5 valour	12 disdain	19 clamour
6 animosity	13 adversary	20 vow
7 conjecture	14 brawl	

TEST 20

1 CEN T R E ASON

2 APA T H Y ME

3 AR E A SEL

4 CAT E R ASE

5 WA V E NOM

6 EARN E S T UARY

7 GO[A][T]TIC

8 WAI[S][T]ARE

9 ID[L][E]GAL

10 PR[E][Y]RIE

11 SE[A][L]LOW

12 FOR[G][E]ESE

13 BAR[R][E][L]AY

14 CAR[P][E][T]AL

15 DEN[S][E]IZE

16 SPO[O][N]ION

17 TA[M][E]AN

18 PR[A][M]END

19 LAP[E][L]EGY

20 COA[C][H]ORE

21 SPI[N][E]EDLE

22 OPA[Q][U][E]UE

23 SI[G][N]AT

24 BA[I][T]CH

TEST 21

1	affect	13	intense	25	temperate
2	contemptible	14	alternative	26	edible
3	definitive	15	distinctive	27	deficient
4	liniment	16	gaol	28	uninterested
5	libel	17	urban	29	emotive
6	testament	18	sanguine	30	negligible
7	complacent	19	illusions	31	officious
8	luxurious	20	credulous	32	strict
9	volatile	21	illicit	33	judicious
10	regrettable	22	inferred	34	masterly
11	conclusive	23	practicable	35	stimulant
12	continually	24	appreciable		

TEST 22

1	bark	10	shuffle	18	log
2	bridge	11	stock	19	grave
3	conduct	12	tramp	20	hide
4	faint	13	bass	21	minute
5	general	14	cape	22	port
6	invalid	15	chest	23	refuse
7	leave	16	crane	24	sound
8	pitch	17	drill	25	strike
9	reel				

TEST 23

Flowers	Herbs	Fish
carnation	basil	cod
cowslip	lovage	haddock
dandelion	marjoram	perch
foxglove	sage	plaice
poppy	tarragon	trout

Kitchen utensils	Tools/Gardening equipment	Containers/ Receptacles
funnel	bradawl	beaker
grater	mallet	caddy
ladle	pliers	crate
spatula	rake	keg
whisk	trowel	skip

Birds	Crimes
budgie	arson
jackdaw	embezzlement
magpie	fraud
starling	perjury
wren	treason

TEST 24

1 – e		9 – o
2 – i		10 – n
3 – f		11 – b
4 – j		12 – g
5 – m		13 – k
6 – p		14 – c
7 – l		15 – h
8 – a		16 – d

TEST 25

Across

3 FOOL	15 ABSENCE	27 HASTE
7 MOLEHILL	17 TUNE	28 SWALLOW
8 PUDDING	19 HONESTY	31 BROTH
9 SERVED	20 MOTHER	32 GAINED
11 STITCH	22 TRICKS	33 LEAP
12 CLOUD	23 FIRE	34 BITTEN
13 EGGS	26 STILL	

Down

1 LOUDER	10 THICKER	21 DESERVES
2 MILK	12 CHARITY	24 BLOWS
4 WILL	14 GIFT	25 HATCHED
5 SLEEPING	16 CHOOSERS	26 SILENCE
6 INDEED	18 HEADS	29 WORM
7 MILE	20 MINDS	30 SIGHT

TEST 26

1 incinerate	10 inaugurate	18 incognito
2 inconsiderate	11 incompatible	19 insatiable
3 indigestion	12 indict	20 incredulity
4 inebriated	13 infuriate	21 incense
5 initially	14 inquest	22 inlet
6 inoculate	15 insolent	23 incentive
7 insolvent	16 innovation	24 innate
8 insipid	17 indispensable	25 incorrigible
9 invulnerable		

TEST 27

	Misprint	Correct word
1	settee	setter
2	fights	flights
3	vandals	sandals
4	speed	speech
5	claimed	climbed
6	stars	stairs
7	pretty	petty
8	nasty	tasty
9	trade	trace
10	writing	writhing
11	roses	hoses
12	diluted	dilated
13	wind	wine
14	fiend	friend
15	conversation	conservation
16	bottom	button
17	prosperity	posterity
18	auctioned	cautioned
19	bear	gear
20	breast	breath

TEST 28

1	discount	11	bullion
2	uninhabitable	12	conducive
3	beforehand	13	exonerated
4	categorically	14	aptitude
5	contaminated	15	sordid
6	indelible	16	ambiguous
7	intersect	17	annuity
8	ratified	18	inevitable
9	vacated	19	disintegrated
10	annihilated	20	trespassing

TEST 29

who's turned over a new leaf (g)
who's on leave (m)
who's cheesed off (j)
who's greasing someone's palm (r)
who's under someone's thumb (a)
who's got the chop (p)
who's in arrears (i)
who's on tenterhooks (n)
who's buttering someone up (d)
who's doing time (e)
who's named the day (o)
who's at a loose end (k)
who's on the dole (b)
who's pulling someone's leg (h)
who's out of sorts (f)
who's for the high jump (q)
who's up in arms (c)
who's blowing his/her own trumpet (l)

TEST 30

1 opted
2 substantiate
3 averted
4 commemorate
5 devastated
6 have fluctuated
7 ingratiate
8 reiterate
9 adjourn
10 cater
11 emits
12 entails
13 jeopardized
14 undermine
15 absconded/has absconded
16 are combing/combed/have combed
17 culminating
18 malign
19 scrutinized
20 allay
21 comply
22 fray
23 exacerbate
24 permeated
25 alleviate
26 commiserated
27 concurred
28 elicit
29 corroborated
30 were incarcerated

TEST 31

	Word a	Word b		Word a	Word b
1	air	heir	21	canvas	canvass
2	cue	queue	22	chord	cord
3	gamble	gambol	23	frank	franc
4	hue	hew	24	isle	aisle
5	medal	meddle	25	pain	pane
6	pair	pare	26	right	rite
7	scent	cent	27	wave	waive
8	toe	tow	28	carrot	carat
9	fair	fare	29	core	corps
10	cast	caste	30	gait	gate
11	coarse	course	31	key	quay
12	oar	ore	32	pore	pour
13	place	plaice	33	cite	site
14	tears	tiers	34	foul	fowl
15	boar	bore	35	loot	lute
16	cymbal	symbol	36	raze	raise
17	gilt	guilt	37	dew	due
18	leak	leek	38	faint	feint
19	pier	peer	39	mare	mayor
20	urn	earn	40	draft	draught

TEST 32

1 EMERALD
2 OCTOPUS
3 CAPITAL
4 HEARSE
5 ADVANCE
6 CORRIDOR
7 REHEARSE
8 PRACTICE
9 ENGAGE
10 DISHONEST
11 TROUSERS
12 BREATHE
13 MANAGER
14 TRAGEDY
15 CHAMBER
16 COCONUT
17 ENGINEER
18 ESCAPE
19 LEATHER
20 CARTOON

TEST 33

1 delinquent
2 invigilator
3 oculist
4 prude
5 stalwart
6 vandal
7 actuary
8 boor
9 expatriate

10	magnate	17	interloper	24	tyrant
11	pallbearer	18	misogynist	25	charlatan
12	punter	19	teetotaller	26	lackey
13	vagrant	20	bigot	27	pawnbroker
14	taxidermist	21	executor	28	squatter
15	adjudicator	22	pathologist	29	convalescent
16	conscientious objector	23	spouse	30	recidivist

TEST 34

1	execute	10	examine	18	expropriate
2	expectant	11	excel	19	extol
3	extension	12	expel	20	excavate
4	extricate	13	exterminate	21	expire
5	exacerbate	14	extradite	22	extremities
6	excise	15	exasperate	23	exclude
7	exonerate	16	exempt	24	excerpt
8	exploit	17	exhort	25	exhume
9	exuberant				

TEST 35

1	passed ... down	8	back ... on	15	feel ... out
2	called ... up	9	tied ... with	16	run ... off/out
3	called ... out	10	got/leaked ... down	17	getting ... away with
4	passed ... round/to	11	run ... through	18	get ... back on
5	turns ... off	12	get ... up	19	coming ... up
6	came ... off	13	carries/goes ... through	20	gets ... after
7	came ... out	14	turn ... out/off		

TEST 36

1	a lion	11	a peacock	21	putty
2	a button	12	a flash	22	a poker
3	the weather	13	a mouse	23	a mule
4	pitch	14	a beetroot	24	thieves
5	a bone	15	rain	25	a rake
6	ditchwater	16	houses	26	old boots
7	pie	17	a dog	27	a kitten
8	a lamb	18	an eel	28	a drowned rat
9	the day is long	19	velvet	29	a sheet
10	Punch	20	a judge	30	an owl

TEST 37

Suggested answers:

1	face	8	holding
2	noticed	9	saying/adage
3	around	10	concerned
4	weight	11	offered/gave
5	connected/linked	12	refused
6	lack	13	offer/gesture
7	convinced/certain/sure	14	noticeable/bad

15 boost
16 attempt/effort
17 life
18 talked
19 actually/literally/physically

20 turned
21 understatement
22 question
23 ever/before

TEST 38

1	backlog	11	correlation	21	antidote
2	counterpart	12	fissure	22	compunction
3	discrepancy	13	prerequisite	23	deviation
4	euphemism	14	quandary	24	figurehead
5	heyday	15	anachronism	25	plaque
6	obituary	16	clemency	26	subsidy
7	referendum	17	conscription	27	effigy
8	Truancy	18	gist	28	infringement
9	adage	19	oversight	29	slick
10	coincidence	20	prevalence	30	idiosyncrasy

TEST 39

1	trifle	10	train	18	rock
2	temper	11	yard	19	state
3	advance	12	approach	20	board
4	change	13	boil	21	charm
5	contract	14	converse	22	corporal
6	habit	15	express	23	row
7	lead	16	incense	24	bolt
8	mould	17	passage	25	desert
9	slight				

TEST 40

1	d	pervade	9	b	Hobson's	16	b	pandemonium
2	c	vested	10	c	travesty	17	a	Shanks's pony
3	c	parson's	11	b	restoring	18	c	facetious
4	d	mollified	12	a	explicit	19	a	a malapropism
5	a	arbitration	13	c	vertigo	20	d	modicum
6	d	snap	14	b	hen	21	b	impervious
7	c	choppy	15	a	frugal	22	b	veracity
8	a	bolt						

TEST 41

1	keep up	10	do away with	18	fallen out
2	laid up	11	keep up	19	put off
3	standing in for	12	let (me) down	20	makes up for
4	look down on	13	fell through	21	gone off
5	butt in	14	fallen off/gone down	22	leave out
6	fix up	15	brought on	23	break up
7	put (me) up	16	kept (you) up	24	died out
8	do up	17	clears up	25	let off
9	puts up with				

TEST 42

19	Across	accidental, caused by chance
28	Across	to fall violently straight down
16	Down	a short, promotional description of a book ...
6	Across	an awkward feeling of guilt, shame or remorse
3	Down	a hidden problem or difficulty
21	Down	to cause something to become black by burning
20	Across	to scold, rebuke
13	Down	thin and hungry-looking
14	Across	a very angry or excited reaction ...
30	Across	goods thrown overboard to make a ship lighter
26	Down	to deliberately insult a person ...
11	Across	a long, heavy rainfall usually causing flooding
7	Down	something that is supposed to be a cure ...
23	Down	enthusiastic applause
25	Across	completely without money or food ...
1	Across	a long wooden seat ...
15	Across	warm and damp
8	Down	to cancel, make void
18	Across	to burn out or clear out the inside of a building
12	Down	to commend, praise
27	Across	a stream which flows into a river
9	Across	a type of large freshwater fish ...
4	Down	a low wall along the edge of a roof ...
5	Across	a sudden strong feeling, for example, of pain ...
2	Down	to run away secretly in order to get married ...
17	Down	the act of taking part with another person ...
22	Across	easily disgusted, excessively difficult to please
10	Down	a model or ideal
29	Across	countless, innumerable
24	Down	a list of goods carried on a ship

TEST 43

1	chain	8	Dutch	15	flat
2	hush	9	inside	16	close
3	pitch	10	dirt	17	bone
4	splitting	11	stone	18	open
5	dead	12	sore	19	French
6	marked	13	confirmed	20	soft
7	casting	14	foregone		

TEST 44

1	creditor	10	cruise	18	crass
2	cremate	11	criterion	19	credulous
3	croquet	12	crib	20	crouch
4	crucial	13	cramp	21	crayfish/crawfish
5	cryptography	14	craving	22	crotchet
6	cradle	15	credentials	23	cravat
7	cranium	16	crypt	24	crank
8	creditable	17	crockery	25	craze
9	crevice				

TEST 45

1	grass widow	11	soft touch	21	lame duck
2	landlubber	12	whizz kid	22	old maid
3	scab	13	brick	23	slavedriver
4	skinflint	14	fence	24	swot
5	tout	15	dogsbody	25	dab hand
6	big shot	16	rough diamond	26	guinea pig
7	chatterbox	17	underdog	27	sponger
8	gate-crasher	18	busybody	28	wet blanket
9	mole	19	dark horse	29	diehard
10	smart aleck	20	grass	30	kerb crawler

TEST 46

	PART	9	TORT	18	BRAG
1	TART	10	TOUT	19	CRAG
2	TARE	11	BOUT	20	CRAM
3	BARE	12	BOLT	21	PRAM
4	BORE	13	BELT	22	PRIM
5	CORE	14	PELT	23	GRIM
6	CORN	15	PEAT	24	GRIN
7	TORN	16	BEAT		GAIN
8	TORY	17	BRAT		

TEST 47

1	de facto	11	ex officio	21	in camera
2	per capita	12	bona fide	22	carte blanche
3	vice versa	13	prima facie	23	curriculum vitae
4	avant garde	14	rapport	24	alfresco
5	faux pas	15	ad infinitum	25	quid pro quo
6	ad hoc	16	détente	26	non compos mentis
7	persona non grata	17	aplomb	27	blasé
8	status quo	18	non sequitur	28	extra-curricular
9	kudos	19	vis-à-vis	29	tête-à-tête
10	coup d'état	20	per se	30	post mortem

TEST 48

1 **b** cows
2 **e** a doctor
(It's the oath made by doctors to try to save life and to follow the standards set for the medical profession)
3 **d** a clump of grass
(a clump of trees, a tuft/blade of grass)
4 **e** a conductor
(It's a copy of music with all the parts for the different instruments on separate lines)
5 **c** to touch wood
(All the others mean to die)
6 **a** a rung
7 **b** stubborn, unyielding
8 **e** the density of gases
9 **b** a turkey
10 **b** wait for no man
11 **b** veins

12   **a**   stagger
13   **e**   a postbox
     (It's a letter-box in a house)
14   **a**   being stared at
15   **a**   a press stud
16   **e**   urn
     (They're all containers)
17   **c**   gannet
     (It's a bird)
18   **c**   a bricklayer
     (He uses it to carry bricks)
19   **c**   sinker
20   **d**   over your shoes

TEST 49

Clothes and accessories
beret
choker
flip-flop
muffler
smock

Diseases/illnesses
catarrh
gout
hernia
mumps
shingles

Insects
centipede
earwig
gnat
louse
midge

Animal sounds
bray
caw
chirp
hoot
whinny

Expressing dislike/hatred
abhor
abominate
despise
execrate
loathe

Smiling and laughing
beam
chuckle
guffaw
smirk
snigger

Taking, holding and pulling
clasp
haul
lug
tow
wrench

Ways of walking
amble
hobble
saunter
strut
trudge

TEXT 50

a
1 – e
2 – f
3 – i
4 – c
5 – j
6 – h
7 – a
8 – b
9 – d
10 – g

b
1 – c
2 – f
3 – a
4 – e
5 – d
6 – h
7 – g
8 – b
9 – j
10 – i

c
1 backbiting
2 bedrock
3 courtship
4 firearm
5 footloose
6 headstrong
7 manhole
8 oversight
9 stopgap
10 windfall

d

1 jingle
2 clatter
3 report
4 blast
5 patter
6 creak
7 rustling
8 clank
9 tinkle
10 lapping

e

1 fatal
2 lucky
3 vivid
4 avid
5 decisive
6 tricky
7 fragrant
8 ingenious
9 ambiguous
10 impenetrable

f

1 – g
2 – d
3 – p
4 – h
5 – n
6 – j
7 – e
8 – a
9 – m
10 – o
11 – l
12 – b
13 – i
14 – f
15 – c
16 – k